Coordinating information and communications technology across the primary school

Mike Harrison

UK The Falmer Press, 1 Gunpowder Square, London, EC4A 3DE
USA The Falmer Press, Taylor & Francis Inc., 325 Chestnut Street, 8th Floor, Philadelphia, PA 19106

First published in 1998

A catalogue record for this book is available from the British Library

ISBN 0 7507 0690 2 paper

Library of Congress Cataloging-in-Publication Data are available on request

Jacket design by Carla Turchini

Typeset in 10/14pt Melior and printed by Graphicraft Typesetters Limited, Hong Kong

Contents

Part two
What IT coordinators need to know

Part three
Developing policy

Part four
Monitoring and evaluation

Part five
Resources for learning

List of figures

Series editor's preface

This book is written for teachers working to improve teaching and learning with and about Information and Communications Technology (ICT) in primary schools. It sets out to help them to make sense of the leadership role they are asked to play and to develop techniques to begin a process which will enable them to take on managerial responsibility for the quality of this work in their primary school. It is recognised that these same teachers will find a need to increase their own knowledge about aspects of IT. This book has therefore been written so that by reading and working on its themes such teachers will be able to begin to establish clear policies for coordinating work amongst their colleagues in their schools.

Why 'ICT'? The assumption is that with the development of the *National Grid for Learning*, aspects of IT communications such as the use of the Internet and electronic mail (e-mail) will increase and so the term 'IT', which is frequently associated with individuals working on solo projects at a computer, will gradually be superseded by 'ICT' which implies a greater use of computers and peripherals for electronic communications. Hence the term ICT is frequently used in this book, although when describing the National Curriculum Programmes of Study, or using quotes from other writers 'IT' will still appear. The Primary IT coordinator has not been renamed, either as ICT coordinator, or as IT subject manager, in the majority of schools. Hence this book will refer to the role using the traditional and well-understood name.

This book forms part of a series of new publications of which I am the series editor. The books set out to advise teachers responsible for providing subject leadership, on the complex issues of improving teaching and learning through managing each element of the primary school curriculum.

Why is there a need for such a series? Most authorities recognise, after all, that the quality of the primary children's work and learning depends upon the skills of their class teacher, not in the structure of management systems, policy documents or the titles and job descriptions of staff. Many today recognise that school improvement equates directly to the improvement of teaching so surely all tasks, other than imparting subject knowledge, are merely a distraction for the committed primary teacher.

Nothing should take teachers away from their most important role, that is, serving the best interests of the class of children in their care and this book and the others in the series does not wish to diminish that mission. However, the increasing complexity of the primary curriculum and society's expanding expectations, makes it very difficult for the class teacher to keep up to date with every development. Within traditional subject areas there has been an explosion of knowledge and new fields introduced such as science, technology, design, problem solving and health education, not to mention the uses of computers. These are now considered entitlements for primary children. Furthermore, we now expect all children to succeed at these studies, not just the fortunate few. All this has overwhelmed a class teacher system largely unchanged since the inception of primary schools.

Primary class teachers cannot possibly be an expert in every aspect of the curriculum they are required to teach. To whom can they turn for help? It is unrealistic to assume that such support will be available from the headteacher whose responsibilities have grown ever wider since the 1988 Educational Reform Act. Constraints, including additional staff costs, and the loss of benefits from the strength and security of the class teacher system, militate against wholesale adoption of specialist or semi-specialist teaching. Help therefore has to come from exploiting the talents of teachers themselves, in a process of mutual support. Hence primary schools have chosen many and varied systems of consultancy or subject coordination which best suit the needs of their children and the current expertise of the staff.

In fact, curriculum leadership functions in primary schools have increasingly been shared with class teachers through the policy of curriculum coordination for the past twenty years, especially to improve the consistency of work in language and mathematics. Since then each school has developed their own system and the series recognises that the one each reader is part of will be a compromise between the ideal and the possible. Campbell and Neill (1994) show that by 1991 nearly nine out of every ten primary class teachers had such responsibility and the average number of subjects each was between 1.5 and 2.2 (depending on the size of school).

These are the people for whom this series sets out to help to do this part of their work. The books each deal with specific issues whilst at the same time providing an overview of general themes in the management of the subject curriculum. The term *subject leader* is used in an inclusive sense and combines the two major roles that such teachers play when they have responsibility for subjects and aspects of the primary curriculum.

The books each deal with:

- coordination — a role which emphasises; harmonising, bringing together, making links, establishing routines and common practice; and
- subject leadership — a role which emphasises; providing information, offering expertise and direction, guiding the development of the subject, and raising standards.

The purpose of the series is to give practical guidance and support to teachers, in particular what to do and how to do it. They each offer help on the production, development and review of policies and schemes of work; the organisation of resources, and developing strategies for improving the management of the subject curriculum.

Each book in the series contains material that subject managers will welcome and find useful in developing their subject expertise and in tackling problems of enthusing and motivating staff.

Each book has five parts.

1 The review and development of the different roles coordinators are asked to play.
2 Updating subject knowledge and subject pedagogical knowledge.
3 Developing and maintaining policies and schemes of work.
4 Monitoring work within the school to enhance the continuity of teaching and progression in pupil's learning.
5 Resources and contacts.

Although written primarily for teachers who are IT coordinators, this book offers practical guidance and many insights for anyone in the school who has a responsibility for the ICT curriculum including teachers with an overall role in coordinating the whole or key stage curriculum and the deputy head and headteacher.

The book's author offers many practical hints and useful advice in order that coordinators can establish and maintain Information and Communications Technology as a central part of the school's intended curriculum. It will help those attempting to develop a whole-school view of the progress children make in ICT and in the way ICT helps children progress across the curriculum. In writing this book I have drawn upon my experience as a teacher educator responsible for the ICT capability and understanding of primary PGCE students, my work as an OFSTED RgI, frequently with responsibility in reporting on IT, and on research, writing and interest in the subject. I hope you will find the book both enjoyable and informative, in that order.

Mike Harrison, Series Editor
June 1998
M.Harrison@man.ac.uk

Part one The role of the IT coordinator

Chapter 1
Contexts for effective coordination

Chapter 2
Developing personal skills and making a start

Chapter 3
Establishing a secure place for ICT in the school

Chapter 1 Contexts for effective coordination

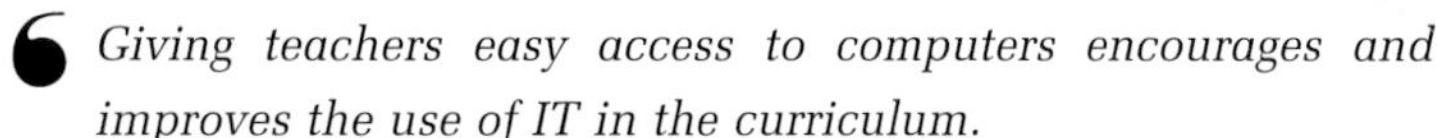

Giving teachers easy access to computers encourages and improves the use of IT in the curriculum.

Research by Cox et al. (1988) and Cox and Rhodes (1988) reported in NCET (1993)

Why do primary schools need an IT coordinator?

The quality of children's work when using computers, as with almost everything else in primary education, depends upon the skills of their classteacher, not in the grandiose plans for management systems, glossy heavyweight policy documents or the titles and job descriptions of promoted staff. Indeed there is an argument to say that the quality of the teacher and their teaching is the key to the educational process and that hence all other tasks are merely a distraction. The role of the classteacher is at the very heart of British primary education, covering all aspects of a child's development and concerning itself with the *whole* child.

This book wishes to take nothing away from that mission. However, the increasing complexity of the primary curriculum and society's expanding expectations, make it very difficult for the class teacher to keep up to date with every development. Within traditional subject areas there has been an explosion of knowledge and new fields have emerged, such as science, technology, design, problem solving and health education, not to mention the uses of computers. These are now considered entitlements for primary children. Furthermore, we now expect all children to succeed at these studies — not just the fortunate few who passed the 11+. 'We have learned that we are no longer prepared to accept an education service in which only a minority prosper' Barber (1994). Further, the National Curriculum has undermined teachers' perceptions about the way in which to implement the curriculum and caused primary teachers to question their personal educational values and professional judgment. All this has overwhelmed a classteacher system largely unchanged since the inception of primary schools after the second world war.

If we accept that primary classteachers cannot possibly be expert in every aspect of the curriculum they are required to teach, surely it is the responsibility of their headteachers to help them. The most important judgment about the worth of your school will be the changes it brings about in its pupils over time. These may be viewed in terms of attitudes, behaviour, respect for elders and property, but mostly by the knowledge and learning children have gained through being in your school.

> *The management of the curriculum may be regarded as being almost identical with the management of the school itself . . . The curriculum remains the centrepiece of school life and its management . . . the main preoccupation of the staff.*
>
> Alan and Audrey Paisley (1989)

Certainly most things are judged as being crucial or peripheral to school life by their level of importance to this aspect of the school and almost the entire productive capacity of the school is geared to this feature. Indeed the quality of our curriculum is our selling point, the focus of our planning, the purpose of staffing, the motivation behind the appraisal process, and will act as an appropriate indicator of the effectiveness of our spending policies.

Curriculum leadership is then surely the main responsibility of the headteacher, especially as they frequently have little or no timetabled teaching duties; in the United Kingdom (UK), unlike some other countries, they are experienced teaching professionals; and the tradition of British schooling is that they command the power to enforce their will. The headteacher is the most influential professional on site, the leadership they offer in Information and Communications Technologies (ICT) as in other curriculum spheres is crucial to the school's educational offering. The National Council for Educational Technology believes 'the attitude of the head teacher is the most important factor in influencing attitudes towards computers and information technology in the school'. Only if the head's attitude is positive will it be reflected in a positive attitude in the other teachers and pupils. They go on to point out that a neutral or detached attitude towards computers is equivalent to a negative attitude, emphasising that headteachers can only give a positive lead in the use of ICT in the curriculum and in the management of the school if they have an understanding of the value and use of ICT themselves.

However, the extended range of roles and responsibilities which headteachers have had to assume since the Education Reform Bill makes it quite unrealistic to believe that they will be able to carry out an effective role in the development and promotion of ICT alongside other curriculum areas. In view of the weight of these responsibilities it is unlikely in theory that teachers will be able to rely on heads alone for the support they need.

> In practise this is borne out as well. Blease and Lever (1992) researched the detailed diaries kept by 25 primary head teachers. They comment '*None of the evidence supports the view that the headteacher fulfils the role of curriculum developer whilst the school is in session. There is little to suggest this takes place out of school either.*' (p. 193)

Some argue that classteachers' difficulties with subject knowledge and curriculum leadership can be solved by the use of secondary style teaching organisation in our primary schools. Classteachers would not need subject help if the teaching was undertaken by a succession of subject experts, they claim. Recent proposals for a National Curriculum in teacher training (Shephard, 1997) maintain that all newly qualified teachers must have a specialist subject as 'too few primary schools have the specialist teachers they need to deliver the 10-subject National Curriculum'. The extent of the need for specialist teaching however, is a matter for debate. Alexander, Rose and Woodhead in their 1992 report, *Curriculum Organisation and Classroom Practice in Primary Schools*, sought to promote several subject specialist roles, the arguments about which will be familiar to most primary teachers. In practice primary schools have not moved *en masse* to specialist or semi-specialist teaching even for the eldest children and certainly not in the core subjects. 'The proposal jars with the fact that primary teachers are (*already*) specialists in their own right' (Wortley, 1993) and several other constraints including additional staff costs, and the loss of the clear benefits to children of the strength and security of the class teacher system, alongside the cross-curricular nature of much primary school work militate against wholesale adoption of such polices. Primary schools, despite a multitude of political pressures still choose the system of consultancy or subject coordination which best suits the needs of their children and the current expertise of the staff.

It is unlikely in any case, that IT will ever have the honour of being taught in a primary school by a specialist teacher, even if it were desirable. IT is mentioned in the preface to each of the subjects of the National Curriculum, it is the most cross-curricular of subjects and with the level of access within each class the computer needs to be working every hour of the working day to be effective in promoting competence for the whole class. One hour a week with a virtual stranger is most unsuitable for this purpose.

For children to succeed without the use of specialist teachers, we need to exploit the talents of teachers in a process of mutual support. As Harrison and Theaker (1989) point out 'a great deal of enthusiasm and expertise in specific curriculum areas has been locked into individual classrooms. It is only when we share knowledge and skills that the true potential of the professional teacher is realised'. Anne Edwards (1993) argues that a policy of using teacher coordinators as change agents in their areas of expertise would allow us to preserve those things which represent the best in primary education such as the class teacher system, the family atmosphere and close contact with parents whilst at the same time adopting whole school curriculum development and effective in-house INSET.

In fact curriculum leadership functions in primary schools have increasingly been shared with classteachers through the practice of curriculum coordination. The Plowden Report proposed that teachers expert in the main field of learning, should give advice to their colleagues throughout the school. Both the Bullock and Cockcroft Reports also promoted the value of teachers acting as coordinators in English and mathematics.

Twenty years ago, the survey *Primary Education in England* showed the many other ways in which posts of responsibility were starting to be used in primary schools to improve the consistency of work in a number of subject areas but particularly in language and mathematics. HMI suggested that 'development . . . will occur most readily when there is a teacher in the school with some specialist knowledge' (DES, 1978). Since then each school has developed their own system of curriculum leadership, a compromise between the ideal and the possible.

By 1988 teachers' terms and conditions of service (DES, 1988) stated that teachers, in addition to their role as a class teacher, should have responsibility for some aspect of the curriculum. Campbell and Neill (1994) show that three years later nearly nine out of every ten primary class teachers had such responsibility and the average number of subjects each was between 1.5 and 2.2 (depending on the size of school). As ICT coordinator you are being asked therefore, to join in a team, sharing your talents and expertise with your class teacher colleagues and benefiting yourself in turn from their efforts by developing your own subject expertise.

In most schools IT coordinators usually combine a generalist classteacher role, with cross-school coordination, advice and support in one or more subjects. It is the skills to be effective in this role which are described in this first part of the book.

Effective IT coordinators have a significant opportunity to improve children's learning in their schools. Meeting the challenge of working with colleagues to produce an effective programme will contribute to personal development and enhance the image of the teaching profession. What is known about the role you will play?

All subject coordinators need to have expertise in curriculum development, management skills, innovation of new ideas and be up to date with current thinking in their area in order to be effective in their schools. The extent to which this can be a reality has been the subject of recent research. In general, coordinators have felt there to be an enormous discrepancy between the rhetoric surrounding the role and the reality of what they were actually able to achieve (Webb, 1994). Bell's (1992) analysis of the results of a self-perception questionnaire showed that at least for science coordinators, while they were prepared to react to requests for help, few felt they could initiate activity to improve colleagues' expertise in science. This is not at odds with others' perception. Moore's (1992) study of headteachers' views of the role of the science coordinator was one where they would talk to colleagues and act as a 'helper' and 'fellow worker' rather than school adviser and decision maker.

Bell (1992) looked at the most common jobs carried out by primary coordinators and showed that there was a high correlation between these ten key tasks, shown here in their rank order.

1. Communicating with the head teacher
2. Exercising curricular leadership
3. Communicating with staff
4. Organising resources
5. Establishing and maintaining continuity throughout the school
6. Organising in-service courses
7. Liaising between head and staff
8. Establishing recording systems
9. Motivating staff
10. Engaging in curriculum development

He went on to group the whole range of tasks subject coordinators carry out under five headings, which have been modified here to reflect the likely work of those with responsibility for ICT. (See The coordinator's role–)

- As an **initiator** a coordinator would:
  - introduce new ideas;
  - develop a school policy;
  - suggest starting points and ideas for school work;
  - develop a stimulating environment.
- As a **facilitator** a coordinator would:
  - provide resources;
  - organise storage, accessibility and use of resources;
  - act as a source of information;
  - be available for discussion and consultation.
- As a **coordinator** a coordinator would:
  - attempt to ensure continuity for pupils within and beyond the school;
  - liaise with outside bodies and other schools;
  - oversee matters of safety;
  - arrange staff discussions and training.
- As an **evaluator** a coordinator would:
  - assess and revise policy and practice;
  - monitor and evaluate the progress of pupils throughout the school;
  - identify appropriate forms of assessment;
  - examine the use and suitability of resources;
  - examine the part ICT plays in the whole curriculum;
  - develop methods of record keeping;
  - record staff development and expertise.
- As an **educator** a coordinator would:
  - help colleagues develop ICT capability;
  - help build up colleagues' confidence;
  - provide guidance and suggestions on the best ways to teach with and about computers;
  - create an awareness of opportunities to use ICT.

The role of evaluator and educator tend to be neglected due to the school culture.

Whole school issues

To be successful in bringing ICT together across the school, senior management will need actively to promote acceptance that the nature of this devolved responsibility implies emphasis upon managerial skill as well as upon curriculum expertise. Thus teachers selected to become IT coordinators will need to develop skills in areas such as the implementation of change, curriculum planning, evaluation and school development, in addition to attending courses about the use of computers and particular software.

IT coordinators will soon discover the importance of understanding and working with the culture of the school. Nias et al. (1989) identified a collaborative culture in the sample of successful schools they examined.

Key elements of this successful atmosphere can be characterised as:

- individual teachers appreciated that they were valued both as people in their own right and for their unique contribution to the teams' work;
- a sense of interdependence in the team;
- personal and professional security led to an openness in the expression of emotion and opinions;
- shared values and goals created a high degree of trust in others;
- a willingness to be flexible and adaptable enabled staff to cope with any uncertainty and crisis.

You may identify with some of the above in your own school and consider some essential elements to be missing in your staff. But, cultures are born and grow. 'Culture is the way we do things and relate to each other around here' (Fullan and Hargreaves, 1992). The crucial factor in the development of an ethos is the nature and attitudes of the people working in and around the school. Of course, **you are one of these people**, whether your influence is for good or ill, and your effectiveness will depend on the way you personally approach the task. Hence by considering your actions carefully you can determine the most appropriate way to ensure progress.

The designation 'team' is widely used in schools, but in reality is usually an aspirational rather than descriptive statement. In a team:

there are explicit, understood and accepted values and vision; the core purpose of the team is clear and unambiguous;

leadership is situational and based upon expertise rather than status;

there is an emphasis on inter-personal relationships;

use is made of problem solving and decision-making techniques;

team processes are constantly reviewed;

there is an emphasis on action.

(after West-Burnham, 1997)

In some schools a contrived collegiality exists and this faces IT coordinators with a difficult situation. Efficient use of time is essential to gain respect and cooperation of colleagues, who will have their own priorities and challenges to cope with. 'Coordinators can only change and develop classroom practice with the active consent of colleagues. In this sense the success or failure of the coordinator is the responsibility of all teachers within the school'. (O'Neill, 1996)

In *The Developing School*, Peter Holly and Geoff Southworth (1989) discuss several other whole-school concerns which will affect the work of subject coordinators. They show that teachers need to be receptive to a collaborative approach and to respect and acknowledge curriculum expertise from within their own ranks. Such an ethos goes hand in hand with an enabling and supportive structure where job descriptions are not highly prescriptive leaving little room for individual enterprise and initiative. Ideally IT coordinators should see that their own job specification is flexible and shows that the school has different expectations of a newly appointed coordinator than from one who has been in post for some time.

Managerial responsibility and support for the coordination of the coordinators must be made explicit. The inspectorate for Northern Ireland point out that

> ❛ *the absence of a clear managerial framework, within which coordinators could meet, plan and evaluate sometimes caused frustration and resulted in less effective coordination than was required.*

Heads must monitor the work of subject managers and offer them guidance at critical times. To whom should you report on your plans, achievements and expectations? If it is not clear, write a report to your headteacher on your initial findings about ICT in the school and ask for a response.

You need to accept that it will take a considerable amount of your time to promote ICT across the school. Yet time is in very short supply in most primary schools. You will need to find time to observe teaching and learning, cope with administration and work alongside colleagues and children in order to effect change. Time will be needed to review software and to organise resources. The lack of time for coordinators was cited by no less than Eric Bolton, when he was Her Majesty's Chief Inspector of schools as a serious obstacle to their ability to work effectively (DES, 1990).

You may find headteachers agreeing with these sentiments but can still provide you with little or no non-contact time to allow you to do your work. Campbell and Neill (1994) show that above the directed time of 33 hours per week, teachers generally believe it is reasonable to spend an additional 9 hours per week on professional tasks. However, this research of teachers' work from four differently selected cohorts of schools and each using different sampling methods shows that they appear to have been spending a total of 52 hours per week in 1991. Thus conscious decisions about how long to spend on each aspect of your workload need to be taken before you can sensibly plan the extent of your coordination activity.

Mike Harrison and Steve Gill (1992), in their book *Primary School Management*, suggest several indicators to show the degree to which any particular primary school supports its coordinators. IT coordinators might consider:

- The **nature of the decisions** they can feel confident in making without recourse to the Head. Does this include calling a quick lunchtime meeting to discuss an ICT issue; ordering on-approval software; trying an experiment with PIPs in three classes; or, asking a hardware representative to call?
- The mechanisms by which **your work as an IT coordinator is to be monitored**. Will you be asked for a report each term/year? Will you be called upon to evaluate the effectiveness of your spending decisions?

- The strength of **the systems in place to support you** as IT coordinator. Will you be able to bid for class release time? Is training available?
- Whether you are **enabled to gain recognition and respect** as a model of good practice in using ICT to good effect, in your classroom and in displays around the school.
- The ways in which coordinators are **encouraged to learn personnel management skills** from one another. Have you had the chance to see other coordinators in action? Do you have a particular teacher on whom you would like to model your management role?
- The degree to which **coordinators are able to work in harmony with the school's stated aims**. Are you being asked to influence the work of other teachers in using computers in accord with the school's ethos?

Thus the culture of the school will define its expectations of you in your role as IT coordinator and when you understand that culture you can influence it and better meet the needs of your colleagues.

> *the major change is about headteacher and classroom colleagues wanting coordinators to have a substantive role, and trusting them to carry it out. The former needs headteachers to delegate authority and responsibility to coordinators and to endorse publicly the role. The latter requires coordinators to demonstrate that they can help individual colleagues to improve teaching and learning in the curriculum area.*
>
> O'Neill (1996)

To work effectively as a coordinator, then, you will have to gain an understanding of the school's needs and its methods for the implementation of the whole curriculum; develop the skills necessary to influence older and more experienced members of staff and be prepared to give time to be on hand to solve the problems of others and eventually pose problems for others to solve. This will take time and you will find that some aspects of this work suit you more than others. Nonetheless, by studying the advice given here, you will go a long way towards being recognised as not only an influential teacher in your school but also as a respected resource of information and skills.

What is expected of an IT coordinator?

With the implementation of the National Curriculum and formal assessment, many class teachers have had to learn new material and develop new techniques which have absorbed a great deal of their attention. Many class teachers therefore may have been unable to exploit fully the potential of information and communications technology in their classrooms as they might. In addition many teachers appointed as IT coordinators have carried this responsibility alongside another major area of the curriculum, so help may not always have been forthcoming in the way needed to encourage teachers to use computers to the full. It has also not always been made clear to them just what they are required to do.

The second follow-up paper to the Three Wise Men Report (OFSTED, 1994) more clearly defined the Generalist/Consultant role, which is the one mostly adopted by primary IT coordinators.

> ‘*In all but the smallest primary schools, headteachers are able to delegate the management of particular subjects to individual members of staff. . . . teachers who are subject managers for the whole school (coordinators is too limited a description) can be expected a) to develop a clear view of the nature of their subject and its contribution to the wider curriculum of the school; b) to provide advice and documentation to help teachers teach the subject and interrelate its constituent elements; and c) to play a major part in organising the teaching and the resources of the subjects so that statutory requirements are covered.*’ (para. 37)

The jobs associated with being a subject coordinator are described in many ways. Webb’s (1994) research shows that ‘the amount and nature of the work fulfilled by coordinators varied enormously from school to school, and often between coordinators in the same school’ (para. 5.9). This is of course just as it should be. In the cycle of curriculum development identified in the school’s development plan, the needs of the school, the varying expertise of staff and the available equipment and materials will mean that different subjects will have differing priorities year by year. If ICT is featured as a priority in this year's School Development Plan (SDP) one might expect the coordinator to undertake a different set of tasks than if it was a major feature in the previous year. The other factor which will presumably be behind the differences found by Webb, will be the nature and length of teaching experience of the appointed coordinator, their level of training, how many years they have been in the school and the desired balance of effort between class teacher and coordinator responsibilities. It will be necessary for you to consider just how much personal time you need to devote to improving the teaching of others and how much to your task of providing for the children in your own class. As many, if not most coordinators, will carry responsibility for more than one subject this too may cause differences in expectations between the job descriptions of various staff.

Such descriptions indicate expectations, give a clue to the range of responsibility and may help you to get a feel for the environment in which you will be working. They do not usually specify the way in which results may be achieved. This has to be done by teachers agreeing together the basis for any changes they want to make. IT coordinators are the means for promoting and implementing these agreed changes in the way computers are used to promote learning and for monitoring pupils' development.

The four main responsibilities of the coordinator are likely to be:

1 policy formation,
2 policy implementation,
3 staff leadership,
4 overall management of resources.

In addition the following responsibilities need to be covered but maybe shared out amongst other staff or by buying in:

purchasing equipment,
technical support,

staff training and general in-house support,
collecting pupils' work and ensuring that it is assessed.

Given the nature of the job it is unlikely that the IT coordinator will be able to function in the future without the following:

- technical skills in using a computer, preferably including detailed knowledge of operating systems;
- skills in the pedagogy associated with the use of information and communications technology;
- organisational skills, both to map the curriculum and to fulfil the demands of the National Curriculum;
- managerial skills to ensure that the best use is made of IT resources;
- inter-personal skills, to ensure that staff feel confident in approaching you for advice.

The purpose of coordinating ICT is to foster the achievement of high standards for the children in the school through good quality teaching and learning. According to class teachers, headteachers, inspectors, and IT coordinators themselves the most common expectations of the IT coordinator are that she will:

maintain and manage the school's ICT policy (including its creation where necessary);

review the provision and care for resources, both hardware and software;

demonstrate good practice in the use of ICT in their own classroom and elsewhere;

arrange the provision of technical support;

give staff advice on software;

attend relevant INSET courses and keep up to date with developments in other ways;

promote, foster (and possibly implement) staff training in ICT;

disseminate ICT information throughout the school;

review ICT practice throughout the school;

liaise with ICT support staff and advisers; and,

regularly review his/her own role and effectiveness.

The role of the IT coordinator is described in many ways with a even wider variation in the aspects of the role which teachers with different levels of experience can or should play.

The particular system of coordination which you will find in the school will also determine the scope of your responsibilities. There is a sense in which IT coordinators define their own role whatever the job descriptions say. What is expected of you as an IT coordinator will be better understood by thinking about whole-school issues than trying to fathom the import of words written on a job description, which really only serves any purpose in times of dispute. Success in acting as a leader has more to do with getting on with people than making systems work, so the next chapter deals with ways to develop personal skills in order to make a good start as IT coordinator.

Chapter 2 Developing personal skills and making a start

Using IT makes teachers take a fresh look at how they teach and the ways in which students learn.

Research by Somekh (1989); Watson (1993) and Ragsdale (1991), reported in NCET (1994)

Personal effectiveness

Success in acting as a leader has more to do with getting on with people than with making systems work. As argued in the previous chapter, the circumstances in which you as IT coordinator find yourself will affect the way you approach the tasks before you. However, the strength of your influence will also depend on the way you personally approach the task. Hence, whether your school situation is ideal or not, by considering your actions carefully you can determine the most appropriate way to ensure progress.

Try to understand how your responsibilities fit into the management structure of the school as a whole. You will be carrying out a delegated responsibility on behalf of the headteacher. Can you establish agreed terms of reference? Can you define the dividing line between a classteacher's autonomy to use or not use the computer and your responsibility to develop and implement a whole school plan? Make sure that you recognise the school's stated central purposes and aims in the work you do and any changes to improve teaching and learning with ICT you are trying to achieve.

To be an effective coordinator your first considerations must be amongst the following:

- How much do you know about the past and present situation and the opinions of the teachers with whom you will be working?
- How clear are you about the changes you want to see in the way ICT is considered, planned, organised, integrated with the rest of the curriculum?
- What will you be satisfied with?
- Are you willing to be fully committed to and involved with colleagues?
- Are you prepared to make the changes yourself?

Key personal skills which coordinators will need to develop in order to promote successful use of ICT within the curriculum, can be listed as:

- an ability to empathise with those threatened;
  Campbell (1985) has described difficulties in the coordinator's role particularly arising from their limited influence in altering their colleagues' classroom practices. Forms of hostility are detected, some of which are linked to a perception by class teachers of a reduction in their own autonomy.
- to act consistently;
  No-one is prepared to follow a leader who chops and changes with the wind and who is so unpredictable that it seems they are never content. Consistency in coordinating ICT might be shown by a willingness to look with teachers at their termly plans; a steady and calm approach to inevitable breakdowns and technical difficulties; timely pursuit of one goal at a time; and praise when teachers succeed in areas they had previously found difficult.
- to maintain hope, belief and optimism;
  The 'can do' approach attracts success with which others will wish to be associated. Those who see the way ahead full of opportunities rather than problems; who see partial success as a result rather than a failure, will win converts. No one likes a moaning pessimistic malcontent. Believe

in your colleagues, look forward to achievements, pursue a positive vision.

- to want success;
  If the target of children's improvement in using LOGO is foremost in your mind, your actions will naturally be geared towards its achievement. If, however, you are not particularly bothered whether or not data bases are used in science, or whether or not Y2 ever do print out their work — it will show.
- to be willing to take calculated risks and accept the consequences;
  Taking risks means being bold in inviting in speakers; making a decision about soft or hardware rather than sitting on the fence; making a strong recommendation to your colleagues; and setting courageous targets for yourself and others. Gain without pain is rare indeed and taking a safe path will mean that your achievements although positive may be moderate. Coordinators need to be fairly thick skinned 'when colleagues performed well the post holder received little credit; when they went badly he or she took the blame' (Campbell, 1985, pp. 68–76).
- to develop a capacity to accept, deal with and use conflict constructively;
  If everything was a smooth route to inevitable improvement, then the computers would currently be seen everywhere being used effectively, all the children would be able to write LOGO procedures and teachers' walls would be covered in high quality work. Your position would not be necessary. If the situation is less than perfect it is quite possible that some people have avoided facing up to modern technology and will continue to do so unless challenged. Who is there to force the issue except you? Conflict may arise. Can you use this effectively?
- to learn to use a soft voice and low key manner;
  This is the antidote to the above. Of course, it is true that persuasion is better than coercion. You will need to cultivate a tolerance of ambiguity and complexity when dealing with colleagues, recognising that issues are seldom black or white. Striking a balance consists of centring on some aspects and being content with partial success in others. The difficult part, of course, is knowing which is which!

- to develop self-awareness;
  Can you find out what others make of your efforts to date? You need to grow to appreciate your own strengths and weaknesses. The willingness of your colleagues to accept advice also depends on their perception of your ability in the classroom. Teachers will also make judgments as to the value of the advice based on the coordinator's range of experience, ability to organise resources, knowledge of the subject and range of interpersonal skills.
- to make strategic compromises;
  Accommodating your expectations to the reality of just what can be achieved is a sign of maturity. An effective compromise, being content to allow some teachers to use just a narrow range of software or employ a limited range of communications technology until they feel sufficiently competent to move on, might be just such a compromise.
- to become an active listener.
  Active listening is merely a matter of approach. Take time to understand the other person's point of view — you need to listen to them as well as stating your own opinions — and then a solution may become apparent.
- to learn to match advice to individual teacher's needs not necessarily your own preferred approach.
  Galton (1995) argues that for in-service training to be effective in changing practice we must approach individual teachers differentially and offer them just enough to help them to the next stage, not overwhelm them with either the best possible practice or the particular approach of the coordinator. Teachers new to the class management issues raised by the continuous use of ICT for example, may not be able to grasp the reasons behind your expert approach to a problem and will put down your success to characteristics such as personality and conclude that the approach is beyond them. Competent and more experienced teachers however may well benefit from involvement with you in their classrooms in the same way that competent musicians improve through attendance at master classes.

This atmosphere can be maintained only where changes introduced are consistently seen to benefit children throughout the school rather than merely to advantage the reputation of the initiator.

Making a start

Before you embark on promotional activities about ICT that you have planned, you need to ask yourself, 'What are people saying about ICT in this school?' You will need to ask questions about the image and standing of work in information and communications technology, how your school's curriculum and provision in this area are currently perceived. You may wish to find out what those outside the school are saying

> *There are various avenues of information ranging from the school gate parliament, local Rotary club, PTA, non-teaching staff and local shopkeepers. None has a monopoly on the truth and it will be necessary to interpret information for its degree of partiality, optimism and pessimism.* (Bowles, 1989)

You may wish to carry out some research externally by eliciting the opinions and concerns of parents. Such an audit should aim to provide you with information about both curriculum development and provision. If we compare ourselves to an industrial or commercial concern then it is the curriculum which is our product on offer. It follows that the educational equivalent to product development is curriculum development. Are there weaknesses in the way children's capabilities in ICT are promoted? What do the governors, non-teaching staff and influential parents believe about the way computers are being used in your school? What would they like to see? Is this realistic? Have you got the balance right between the different uses of computers and other ICT work and between its use and other important features of school life? Do parents feel that there is too much of one thing and not enough of another? Are there extra-curricular ICT activities parents would like to see? How do professionals feel about justifying their decisions to parents on these matters?

There are two effective ways of finding out such opinions.

A questionnaire

1 It is the more likely that respondents will answer yes/no questions than construct written answers. Yes/no answers are also easier to analyse.

2 Answers may be the more honest if the questionnaire is anonymous.
3 Accentuate the positive qualities of the school in the questionnaire.
4 Make the completed forms the entry for a raffle or give some other sort of incentive to maximise the number of questionnaires returned.

A discussion group

Discussion groups are useful for generating ideas or for going into issues in more detail. Ideally, you need to form groups of seven or eight. A balanced group is very important here because you need a broad and balanced view of the school's perceived strengths and weaknesses, not just the views of the vociferous minority.

A starting point for discussion might be comments on the results of the questionnaire. Responses are the more likely to be valid if the group leader is not someone with a vested interest in the school. In either case one thing has been proved: you are showing your community that you are interested in and are actively measuring the perception of the use of ICT in school. The impact of any policy may be small, but if you are seen to be interested in improvement this may be more influential than the policy changes themselves.

You will also need to carry out an internal audit. You will need to find out: how frequently:

children use computers in various classrooms;
printers, roamers, CD ROMs are used;
pupils use their e-mail addresses;
children have access to open-ended software;
children are able to choose whenever or not to use the computer?

What variety:

of machines are in use;
of software exists;
of Web sites are visited;
of software is known to teachers;
of work is displayed in the school?
(see Figure 2.1)

Record of Computer equipment in school					
Hardware and peripherals	Where sited? Who is responsible	Model and Serial no.	Bought (date) warranty	Where purchased? and Price	Condition/Comments/ Repairs/Cost of repairs

FIG 2.1
Computer equipment audit form

What levels of competence are demonstrated:
by children;
by different sexes;
by different ability groups;
by teachers?

Find out how much ICT work is going on. Do displays around school show that mathematics is seen as more than just sums in books and that the computer has a part to play? Can you see a variety of graphs and spreadsheets being displayed? Does children's computer art work feature in assemblies? Do teachers talk about progression in children's information or communications technology skills at breaks or in staff meetings? Does the use of ICT feature prominently in work labelled under another subject? Do pupils make visits to places of interest in cyberspace before going there on foot (or in a coach)? Identify where teachers place ICT in their curriculum planning forecasts. By considering such questions you may begin to develop a feel for the task ahead.

This can be followed up by an examination of your school's strengths, weaknesses, opportunities and threats in this curriculum area (SWOT for short). This needs to be applied to every aspect of ICT in school and should ideally involve all staff. An internal audit will seek to assess the strengths and weaknesses of work with ICT in the school and the opportunities and threats offered by its environment. A number of suggested strategies to enable you to secure this information can be found in Kotler and Fox's book *Strategic Marketing for Educational Institutions* published in 1985.

A **SWOT** analysis checklist might consist of:

Strengths
The things your school is good at in the field of computers.

Good pupil capability in KS1/KS2, innovative teaching using programmable robots; good community links with local helpers contributing to the work; strong inter-school communication through e-mail or video links; teachers committed to helping children to develop capabilities in this area, development of the school's own Website; good resources, facilities, peripherals and appropriate software; staff willing to share successes and failures in teaching a variety of concepts by the use of computers.

Weaknesses
The things which let your school down and hold children back from achieving their potential in ICT.

> *Staff members who do not recognise children's entitlements in this area of work; staff reluctant to try new approaches; lack of a culture which encourages practical, problem solving approaches to learning; poor progression in ICT skills through the school; poor facilities in space or the quantity or quality of hardware; limited electrical sockets and bad placement of computers; poor use of ICT equipment; poor behaviour of children on the computer or using peripherals outside the classroom; books, paintings and rubbish piled on top of computers in the classroom.*

Opportunities
Your school's potential for the successful development of work in ICT.

> *New educational opportunities you can foresee; commercial sponsorship for ICT equipment; ICT development projects in the locality; new ideas nationally or from local advisory staff; ICT as a priority in SDP; the starting up of a local coordinators' support group, course opportunities, new appointments of teachers with fresh ideas.*

Threats
Potential problems your school faces.

> *Aging machines and no will to replace them; yet another national initiative; loss of key staff; local indifference to the use of computers, competition from neighbouring schools with much better ICT facilities; thefts and vandalism.*

Identify two or three specific points in each of the SWOT categories — more than this will confuse the issue. When you have completed the analyses of the survey you should have a clearer picture of your strengths in depth and have started to identify areas in need of attention.

Such a SWOT analysis can be a useful way to discuss with staff the present situation and the tasks ahead of you all. A force field analysis might also be used to get your colleagues to identify and work on aspects of their provision with an intent of overall improvement.

Your task together is to attempt to maximise the positive and diminish the effect of the negative influences. Once out in the open this is more easily accomplished.

FIG 2.2
Force field analysis

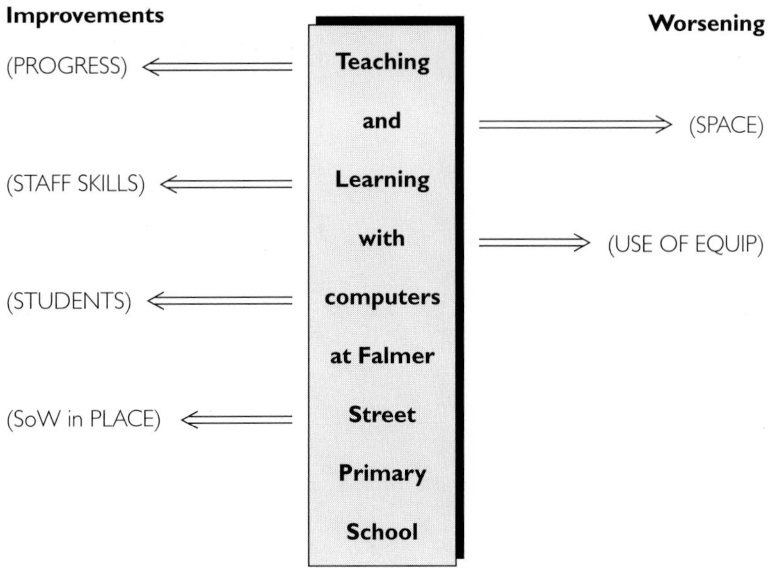

Subsequent to such a meeting, start to think in terms of planning your approach. In order to write this plan try to write a statement which will act as an aim. It may help if you try to state the aim in one simple sentence. Write down all the relevant words and phrases and then get them down to one statement. Consider the ways that your aims might be realised and make a note of these. Divide up your list and say whether these can realistically be achieved, tackled or addressed in the long, medium or short term. This should put you in a position to make some clear statements of intent and a possible order in which to tackle them. This has to be seen as a working agenda and can only be presented as your personal thinking so far. In later stages you will allow others to influence your thinking and the course of events.

Work with staff to create a statement of intent which may be as simple as any of the following:

By Christmas in every year children will have rehearsed and, where possible, extended the range of skills mastered in the previous year.

We believe that children at Falmer Street Primary deserve a thorough grounding in the full range of applications suitable for children of their age.

In every class children deserve maximum exposure to the full range of applications on the computer.

We intend to ensure that children's word processing skills are developed to the full.

By encouraging children to use the Internet the school intends to emphasise that computers can help children seek and retrieve information from all over the world.

By setting appropriate challenges and maximising the time children spend on the computer we expect children to develop strong skills in the use of a variety of applications.

By the time children leave this school they will all be confident competent computer users ready to face challenges . . .

Some action points for you as coordinator may stem from your audit.

Set up a recording system for yourself where you keep your notes, relevant documents and begin to keep a diary. This will help you to show development and progress over time and to demonstrate your success. Talk to the headteacher in order to discover the head's thoughts and commitment to the promotion of ICT across the school; determine its current priority within the school development plan; register your interest and commitment to the task in hand; negotiate the next step and hence formulate a rationale and targets for your work.

Find out about the latest advice from the British Educational Communications and Technology Agency (BECTA — previously NCET), the Qualifications and Curriculum Authority (QCA — previously SEAC) or DfEE. Have you read what OFSTED have to say about inspecting IT? Make contact with a local adviser, advisory teacher, school, college or university where advice may be available. Take note of any courses which might help you or your colleagues. Enquire about any national association such as MAPE (Micros in Primary Education). Do they have local meetings? Might your head pay for you to go to their national conference (usually held over the Easter weekend). How does the local community fit in? Are there people within your community with interest or expertise in the use of computers or who have time to help children develop their skills in this area?

Ask to control and account for a small budget (see Figure 2.3) to support your promotion of ICT. You will then be able to buy and use soft and hardware resources without continual recourse to your head teacher. Arrange to find a method of gaining agreement amongst the staff for the use of this money.

Coordinator's name: ____________________ Report to: ____________________

Allocation allowance £ ____________________ GEST component: £ ____________________

Year: ____________________ Previous allowance record completed Y/N ____________

IT Coordinator's budget record Sheet no: ____________

Date	Order reference	Amount before vat	Running total GEST ALLOWANCE	Delivery date	Items outstanding	Invoice number and date	Passed for payment	Storage location	Usefulness of purchase after 1 year

FIG 2.3
Budget record sheet

Record the results of any meetings (formal and informal) you have had to determine spending of this fund and include this record with an end-of-year account of what the money was spent on. Give this in to the head even if she doesn't ask for it. Can you make a judgment as to the value for money spent in last year's budget? Was the ROAMER of more use than the CD-ROM drive? Which software was the most welcomed? Should you have bought two black and white printers rather than the colour one? Make sure that you show that you have considered such issues when you write up your report on last year's spending.

Provide 'first aid' technical help. In no other area of the curriculum does there exist the degree of confusion between the role of teacher with that of technician. IT coordinators are indeed unique in the demands made upon them for technical support and know-how. It is rare for the maths coordinator to become involved in repairing maths equipment, or the geography coordinator to be called out of class in an emergency to mend the globe. Yet time after time, those with responsibility for ICT seem to be expected to know what to do when someone in Y2 has put a biscuit in the disc drive, provide an instant solution when the discs have been dropped in the fish tank or Johnny's LOGO pattern will not print. In the first few years of using communications technology you may be held responsible for pupils' failure to connect to desired Websites or when e-mails get lost. At an early stage you will need to decide how you intend to react to such requests. More than one coordinator has been asked to leave her class to see to a computer, connect to a turtle, solve a disc problem. Work out beforehand what *you* will do. My advice is not to contribute to some teachers' learnt helplessness. Send a polite but helpful message back, while refusing to leave your children unattended. Normal lesson preparation includes making sure that the equipment needed, be it paper, paint, PE apparatus or floor turtles, are in place and in working order. Teachers may need to be encouraged to think well in advance in order that the time at which you may be needed for consultation and even emergency action will be one where you may be free to give assistance. Acting consistently is the key. Once staff have come to expect you to provide instant solutions to all of their problems then your refusal may be interpreted as a snub.

There is, of course, a case for having someone on the staff who has taken the time and trouble to learn to cope with some of the technical matters that can get in the way of using computers efficiently. That someone is you.

Manuals and guidebooks should be read and important matters highlighted, so that the attention of other readers will be attracted to essential information. Where I believe you should draw the line, however, is whenever a screwdriver is needed. Unless you are familiar with the maintenance of electronic devices, leave anything which involves tools and dismantling parts of the machine to those paid to know such things. Should an accident occur as a result of your untrained experimentation inside a machine, it will be no-one's fault but your own.

You will need to **find out what sort of arrangements have been made in the past to repair broken computers**, upgrade to higher specifications, install chips and to give advice on the running of programs. Your school may have a contract with a local firm or an arrangement with the LEA. You can make the resolution of technical problems as smooth as possible by supplying teachers with the appropriate forms to report problems and occasionally checking yourself to see if all the computers are in working order. In a few cases, teachers reluctant to use ICT may not report malfunctions in good time. In such cases it is the children who are being denied their entitlement. Your timely, polite and efficient work in this area can minimise disruption to their progress.

Find out what **individual strengths** there are amongst the staff. This is where we ask children to start from. It is not unreasonable that we should display this good practice in a management situation. Look out for and **exploit the range of their ICT competence**. Some teachers will be skilled at making computer generated worksheets, some make very good use of class management and organisation to maximise children's use of the computer; under the tutorage of other teachers children become peer tutors to others in their class; and, in yet other classes teachers get children to make class newspapers, display work for all to see or build data files of children's details which would be of use to others in the school. Your job is to coordinate and this means to spread this good practice wherever possible. Get these teachers on your side and encourage them to share their successes.

Look further and ask questions, listen to whether colleagues talk about work in ICT. Will they talk to you about it? Talk to the headteacher to determine his/her attitude. Examine school documentation of all kinds. Are there reference books on the use of computers in industry, commerce and for leisure in the school library? Find out whether there have been previous initiatives in promoting ICT. How have colleagues responded to change in the past?

You will, sooner rather than later, need **to arrange to go into other teachers' classrooms** to work with them. Consider the reasons you will need to give teachers for your presence. Are you to be there as a critical friend; to focus on an area of ICT the teacher has identified; to discover the quality of the outcomes when using the computer or to give you an idea of progression in children's word processing skills across the school? Should you report what you find in other teachers' classrooms? Who is to have access to this information? Decide before you start; there should be respect for colleagues' privacy.

It may help you to **invite outsiders in** to run a short session or to discuss your findings of the state of ICT in the school at present. LEA advisers, other teachers, educational consultants, local university staff, might all prove good sounding boards. Many local authorities have advisory teachers who can be used in this way. Outsiders can have a range of effects. They can present new ideas and provide you with a more objective view, but it is important that these outsiders have something to offer, are credible and are prepared to listen to you and your colleagues. Talk to people you know and respect professionally. Who do they recommend?

Some IT coordinators have found it useful to arrange a **visit to a local school**. This might be just for you, you and your head or the whole staff. Choose the school carefully as sometimes there are petty rivalries between local schools. Avoid authority show-schools, as it is easy for teachers to resent other teachers who have already resolved their problems. The best school to visit is one where the corresponding coordinator is like-minded and where they face challenges of a similar order such as few resources, lack of expertise, lack of confidence. During the visit focus your attention on one or two aspects as well as getting an overall impression.

Use a 'ghost' such as a person, body or event outside the school. This can be effective in starting a process of change if you are new to the post. It is an unassertive way to start the ball rolling and if it suits your style use the government, the LEA, a local initiative, OFSTED: all may usefully be cited as the force behind the need to make a particular change. Be aware that this can also breed resistance.

Advice is given in the next chapter about organising a **series of staff meetings and/or a professional development day** and specific events. It is likely that such meetings will be the core of any discussion that your teachers are involved in, particularly in the early stages. They must be planned with care, one successful one is far better than a series of events which lead nowhere.

You will need to **tackle classroom management issues at an early** stage. There are few issues to do with the curriculum which do not impinge on classroom management and ICT is no exception. It is the matter which leads most frequently to the failure of change in the classroom. Teachers are often wary of describing their classroom management. They may feel that they will be judged as formal or inflexible. Avoid descriptions which emphasise polarities, such as — structured or unstructured, didactic or discovery methods, child-led or teacher-led. These do not serve to unite colleagues. The most realistic start along this road might be to say that you recognise that there are a multiplicity of approaches and professionals select those which are most appropriate. However, we have to make clear to the teachers around us that no-one has the right to be an island because children pass from one class to another. Hence consistency and continuity demand some common practice.

All teachers have **children's learning as a common goal**, so use it. Ask colleagues how their children might react to an activity. If you know the children it may be useful to refer to individuals. Ask colleagues about the range of abilities in their group. Encourage teachers to bring children's work which has been enhanced by the use of ICT, along to meetings. Also **use literacy and numeracy as common reference points** as these aspects of the curriculum are common to all age groups and teachers have a real desire to develop them. ICT enhances children's learning in these areas and it is important to stress this.

A resource base is something that you can develop from day one. You may have little in the way of funds but invariably you can make a start by establishing a resource for teachers and children to use. This will have several effects. It will help to establish that you are the coordinator, that the job needs doing and that doing the job has direct benefits to your teacher colleagues.

Set attainable goals in small steps, like asking teachers to use a new simple resource may lead through success to larger strides. Teachers who experience failure are sometimes very hard to re-motivate.

Strong personal relationships with colleagues may help or hinder your initiatives. Friendly or not, you must strive for a professional relationship. **Being a professional friend** means you can trust one another with teaching and learning as the focus of relationships. In order to build such a relationship you may have to demonstrate your skills and admit to one or two personal weaknesses.

Some colleagues will absorb all of your energy and give you nothing in return so you need to learn to **avoid these bottomless pits**. You have limited time and cannot afford to devote it to lost causes, but in time they might approach you in order not to be left out of the exciting developments being undertaken by their colleagues. This is not an excuse however to ignore those teachers who might well have doubts, those who feel insecure with the changes you are instigating and who are not immediate converts. These teachers are your challenge, the reason you have the post you hold. It is by the changes in **their** behaviour you will be able to measure your progress.

Remember as IT coordinator you are bound to get plenty of ups and downs. If you can **act like a swan** then even in the most difficult of times you will appear calm and tranquil on the surface even if actually paddling like mad underneath.

In addition to whole school pre-requisites, your own personal skills and attitudes will, of course, greatly influence your level of achievement. Management at all levels is predominantly about interpersonal relationships. Thus IT coordinators need to consider the range of their interpersonal skills and how to get their messages across.

Effective communication

Some IT coordinators may find that their opportunities to influence colleagues is limited. The lesson we all learn, when dealing with adults, is that to be effective we need to understand that the method we use to get our messages across may be just as important as the content itself.

It may help to be reminded of some guidelines for effective communication. The following list is based on the principles in Joan Dean's book *Managing the Primary School* (1987).

- Teachers are more likely to be responsive to the advice of coordinators if addressed personally rather than anonymously in a staff meeting or by memo. The coordinator who claims, 'No-one is using the computer enough', in a staff meeting not only is ineffective in rousing the reluctant to switch on the computer but may have also succeeded in alienating the teachers who conscientiously plan to involve all their children in ICT work across the curriculum. These are just the people you need on your side.
- Coordinators will need to learn that with teachers, just as with children, rousing the interest of the listener is necessary in order to get their message across.
- Information is more likely to be valued if it gives an advantage in power or status to the listener. *'I'd like to show you how to drop DRAW files into PenDown after school. Your children will be able to produce illustrated accounts of their outing for display on parents' evening'.*

- No-one likes to be seen as letting down their team or working group. It is desirable therefore sometimes for coordinators to present their information in such a way that it requires action upon which others will rely. *'Perhaps the Y3 and Y4 teachers could bring some computer generated art work to the next meeting'. 'Would you discuss with your head of department the ways ROAMER has worked to emphasise aspects of the maths programme?'*
- Teachers charged with the responsibility of promoting curricular areas to their colleagues may find an advantage in choosing an appropriate messenger. The status of the source of the information is often seen to indicate its importance. For instance ask the head to get teachers to label their work for parents' evening.
- The situation (surroundings, time of day etc.) should be chosen carefully in order to predispose the listener to be receptive. While teachers are on the way to the staff room is not the best time to get them to consider a new initiative.

Making meetings effective

Meetings are the most common method that IT coordinators use in an attempt to get their message over, however these are not always a success. Just having a meeting is not enough. The prime consideration must be 'What do you want to happen at the meeting?' This point is seldom addressed, for many meetings need never happen at all.

You may need to call a meeting:

- to communicate information
  As IT coordinator you will often need to give information to your colleagues, such as the dates and location of a local computer exhibition, the list of programs bought by the PTA and so on. Often this information can be given out in written form with only a brief explanation needed, possibly without having a meeting at all. The skill you will need to develop is to ensure that the information is read and acted upon. Wasting every one's time for an hour, to compensate for your lack of foresight in not preparing a briefing sheet however, does not go down well with busy teachers.

Suggestion

- Why is the meeting being held?
- Who needs to be there in order to achieve this?
- What will each person at the meeting do?
- When is the time most likely for participants to respond to your needs?
- Where is the most appropriate place for the meeting to be held?
- How will any decisions be reached?

- to generate discussion
  If you want teachers to discuss issues, they need to have been properly prepared beforehand by being given the relevant information. You may need to arrange the seating in such a way that everyone can see each other in order to encourage participation. A brainstorming session recorded on tape can generate ideas or possible solutions.
  The key to success for this type of meeting is to create an atmosphere which encourages staff to share ideas and perceptions. They will not do this if early statements are not accepted at least as starting points for the generation of further ideas.
- to make corporate decisions
  If you are organising a meeting to reach a decision on a key topic it is vital that everyone is made aware that the meeting has this as its purpose. Time has to be allowed beforehand, such that small group meetings can already have aired some of the issues. Make sure teachers have had time to read and absorb printed material or tried out software. Decide before the meeting if you intend to take a vote should it prove necessary, or whether it would be more appropriate to continue the debate until a consensus has been reached.

IT coordinators will be more effective if they understand the difference between the various purposes of these staff meetings and realise what can go wrong. We have all attended meetings that were monopolised by one person, had too many important items left to the end, or failed to get people involved. We have also all attended well-run friendly and relaxed meetings which kept to the point and seemed like time well spent. You need to consider a variety of strategies for organising and chairing meetings (cf. Suggestion).

25 ways to kill a good idea

As part of your role you will have transmitted a vision of the ways in which children's learning can be enhanced by the use of computers in the classroom. Despite what is said in the staffroom it is unlikely that everyone will share your vision and before long you may need to remind your colleagues of what they agreed. You might wish to challenge them to put this into action.

One such challenge is to organise a meeting in which every possible objection to your idea is already out in the open. You have thought up the objection — challenge the others to think up the response! Such a list might look like this:

We teachers don't know enough about ICT.
Show them!

The computers always go wrong whenever we use them.
Always?

We tried all this before but . . .
With enthusiasm?

Our children aren't clever enough to use computers properly.
Prove them wrong

We've not got the right software/printers/CD ROM/robots.
They probably have!

Computers will always be too expensive to do the job thoroughly.
But we can make a start with what we've got.

When on the computer children are missing other vital work
Use ICT to do the same thing, but more effectively

Children in this school don't cooperate well enough to use the computer in pairs.
Show them how to.

I've nowhere to put it.
Make a suggestion

We only do word processing in this school.
Not any more!

We've run out of ink/paper/and can't use the printer.
Check your supply and repair system

Its good in theory but can never work in practise
Get staff to visit another school where it does work.

There are better non-computer ways to learn the same thing.
Then don't do that with a computer, use it for what it does best.

They've all got computers at home.
Good, then capitalise on this and use their skills for educational purposes

The parents won't like it.

Rubbish

You haven't considered . . .

Ask the objector to consider it

Let's not step on the toes of the secondary school

Let's give Y6 a good start when they go to their next schools

You don't understand our problems here.

Get them to tell you

Let's make this a priority next year.

. . . but make a start in this

Why start anything new this late in the term?

. . . to get ready for next term

We're too small to be good at everything.

Our children deserve the chance to be good at something

The new teachers won't be able to do it.

Try them

We have too many other initiatives right now.

. . . and you think the demands upon us will diminish in the future?

Let's try it out in one class for a year

. . . and let the other children try some of it

Let's wait until after the next inspection.

. . . when IT will certainly be on the action plan if you do nothing now!

Getting the teachers themselves to come up with counter arguments is the most productive route.

Chapter 3 Establishing a secure place for ICT in the school

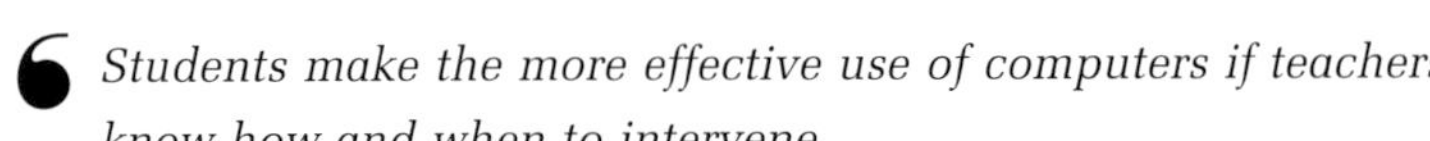

> *Students make the more effective use of computers if teachers know how and when to intervene.*
>
> Research findings Fisher (1993); Hill (1990) and Hoyles and Sutherland (1989) reported in NCET (1993)

Promoting lasting change

Change is an interesting area of human experience. Attitudes to it tend to be self-perpetuating. It is almost always the case that the individual who dislikes change will have difficulty accepting it and will rarely be totally positive about its results. The attitude of the participants seems to be the most influential factor in its successful implementation.

IT coordinators would do well to consider what is commonly described as the change equation when attempting to propose initiatives.

It is an important feature of this function that for the left hand side to be positive each of the terms individually must be positive, for if any term is zero then however large the others

FIG 3.1
The change equation

dissatisfaction with the current situation	×	a shared vision of the future	×	knowing the first steps	>	the resistance to change

Suggestion

Know where you want to go and unite the team with this vision.
Create in the minds of the people with whom you work the need for that change.
Help people to diagnose problems and to discuss them openly.
Value teachers and promote their professional growth.
Develop a risk-taking mentality.
Make change incremental.
Try to avoid surprises.
Create opportunities for groups to interact.
Commit yourself to continuous improvement.
Avoid the extremes of euphoria over success or completely defeated by failure.

the result will always be zero. Thus, for change to take place in your school, IT coordinators will need to create or exploit teachers' dissatisfaction with what they are doing at present; attempt to create an image of what advantages to children and teachers the proposed change will mean; and, convey some idea of the steps which will need to be taken.

Resistance to change which will need to be diminished include:
fear of the unknown;
lack of full information;
threat to core skills and competence;
threat to status;
no perceived benefits;
low trust in the school as an organisation;
poor relationships between staff;
fear of failure in implementing agreed work;
fear of looking stupid because of lack of ICT skills.

Coordinators therefore need to persuade, cajole and affect the attitudes of staff toward:

- the need for change;
- the focus of the change (for example the frequency of use/an aspect of ICT);
- the change process itself.

The options and strategies outlined here will therefore focus upon the process and personal considerations involved when coordinators seek to influence the teaching behaviour of others.

Most teachers do support change. They want the effect of their efforts to the maximised and to teach as effectively as possible, but change will never be achieved solely as the result of your plan, government legislation or incidental INSET. Real and permanent change only occurs when teachers believe in the need for it, know where it is going, are committed to it and have some ownership of it. (cf. Suggestion)

Acting as a resource for your colleagues

The most crucial part of your role is that in which you motivate, cajole and persuade staff to work together in ICT just

Think about

In order to gain the support of colleagues IT coordinators have:

- organised INSET days;
- arranged regular times to be available for consultation;
- supported teachers' own applications to attend INSET;
- put on demonstrations at lunchtimes;
- advised at team/year group curriculum planning meetings;
- checked and commented on teachers' termly work forecasts;
- worked alongside teachers in their classrooms;
- arranged visits to other schools to see IT in action;
- arranged for the loan of computers for teachers to use at home;
- put up displays of children's IT work; and,
- arranged software loans for trials.

as in any other part of the curriculum. Your best indicator of performance as a coordinator will be the extent to which you achieve such objectives. There are a number of formal and informal ways to induce staff to cooperate.

Whole-school INSET days can allow staff to have time to discuss the way ICT is being used and have access to new machines and a variety of software. Visiting speakers bring a new perspective on the value of activities, and frequently say things that you may not be able to say. Problems may be discussed which were not previously aired, issues may arise involving different areas of the school, and unthought of cooperation may result.

INSET days can be used as opportunity for new beginnings and therefore must be properly thought out to maximise their effectiveness. Any guest speaker will need to be properly briefed on the current activities of the school. Some suggestions for the best use of INSET time can be found later in the chapter.

Incidental INSET can arise from time to time in which you have the opportunity to show individual teachers features of a machine or software. These opportunities occasionally arise in the solution of everyday problems, but they may also come from a deliberate tactic on your behalf to be in the right place at the right time. Some coordinators have been successful by setting up a computer in the staff room at lunchtime once a fortnight. Such occasions could consist of a demonstration by you of a piece of software or just an opportunity for individual staff, at their leisure, to try out something with you close at hand to give assistance (cf. 'Think about' box in left-hand column).

Whichever methods of training have been used in the past they have not always been as effective as many would like in persuading teachers to use ICT to support children's learning across the curriculum (Harrison, 1994). As discussed in an earlier chapter, Galton's conclusion was that whatever assistance you proffer it needs to be closely matched to the needs of the recipient rather than merely reflect your own preferences. Failures to implement new curriculum reform through the use of coordinators may not be due to poor subject knowledge or lack of counselling skills but an inability to match training offered to the cognitive state of the learner. It could be that the steps teachers have been asked to take are just too big and they have been asked to take them far too quickly. Jane Devereux (1991) suggests that for some children '. . . the use of other, more familiar technology might provide a safer, smaller step for those children a little daunted by the computer itself'. She goes on to show ways in which IT other than computers can be used to support primary science. Perhaps such simpler steps might commend itself to some coordinators trying to help teachers who are over-faced by technical complexities.

It has also been argued that the problem of INSET has been the deficit model it has used. The deficit model says to teachers

> *You lack certain technical knowledge and skills. Come on this course and I will show you how to connect up to an internet search engine; configure this machine; run this program.*

Such training has largely been characterised by telling participants which button to press and when, and how to operate accessories. It has not called upon the professional experience of teachers, nor used their motivation to help children learn, which is their first calling. Because of this it has been less effective than it might have been.

An alterative model which is beginning to be seen as more successful, however, concentrates on building the need for ICT and presents the use of a computer as a solution to teachers' own problems. Thus as well as some technical help and training the core of the effort should be in them helping teachers to understand how ICT can support children's learning in various areas of the curriculum. Thus attending topic planning meetings to suggest the appropriate use of computers as the teachers' needs arise, looking at forecasts of teachers' work and showing ways in which the use of computers can help them to achieve their own ends, is likely to be more effective and longer lasting, than any amount of technical instruction.

Whether you feel confident enough to work in such a way or not these further ideas may commend themselves to you as your career develops. You could arrange for staff to visit schools in the district with a brief not to centre on the technical wizardry of the resident teachers, but to see if their use of ICT proffers any solutions to your teachers' problems such as, individualising work for certain children, handling information in pie charts and graphs, empathising with children of the past, helping children understand the movements of the planets, creating perfectly lettered 3–D titles to show off children's work.

You could obtain 'on approval' software for teachers to try out in their own classrooms and ask them to write a few words on whether it helped with their class work. You will display infant computer work in the juniors' and vice-versa to demonstrate its value in different areas of the school.

Thus it is in utilising teachers' already existing desires to serve their children to the best of their ability that the source of motivation may lie (see Figure 3.2).

Running an INSET day

IT coordinators are often concerned that they have had no training in organising a professional development day for colleagues. Yet such an event can enhance your own status and may be an effective way of emphasising the progress the school is making in using ICT across the school.

If given time in a staff meeting or a non-pupil day, Cross and Cross (1994) give a range of advice on how you should begin your preparation and clarifying its purpose. What do you feel the school and your colleagues need to get out of the day? Talk with colleagues, and seek advice from the deputy and headteacher for detailed guidance. You could prepare and circulate a simple proposal for the day telling everyone that you want feedback to prepare and ensure that good use is made of the time available.

Once you are more clear about the training day you can start to think about the nature of the activities you might wish to include.

Development Priorities in ICT

Term: ______________ Year: ______________ Coordinator: ______________

Action Plan items in order of importance	Key staff to work with	Training provider: and costs	Planning/development duration	Hardware and software: costs	Expected learning benefits

FIG. 3.2
Establishing priorities in ICT

Suggestion

One way to start a non-pupil day is to prepare an information sheet to introduce teachers to an area of ICT or an aspect of learning with which they may be unfamiliar. This may stimulate discussion and provide a context for the session. Real examples of classroom practice may provide activities for groups, individuals or pairs to work through.

Make sure that:

- everyone knows the arrangements, including part-time and temporary staff;
- non-teaching staff are aware of what is happening;
- any printing is done well in advance of the day, with extra copies of everything;
- the room will be large enough, the right temperature and comfortable (small chairs can cause great discomfort!);
- any documents required will be available;
- stationery is on hand;
- videos and computers work — check them the previous day and again immediately before you start;
- lunch arrangements are made and agreed.

- An introduction
  What will you say at the beginning of the session? Perhaps a simple statement of your aims; something about yourself, if you are fairly new to the team; whom you have consulted about the planning of the day; an outline of the activities you have planned. Be sure to tell everyone about the timing of breaks — and stick to them! (cf. Suggestion box)
- Practical work with computers, Roamers etc
  Consider the way you will introduce any new software. Remember that teachers have to be won over so your selling point is to emphasise the benefits it will bring the children. Can you show results from your own classroom? The purpose of this section of the day has to be to make your colleagues **want** to use this in their classrooms — and consequently try their best to learn to use the application. You may try to introduce them to research on the Internet.
- Brainstorming
  There may be a genuine need to seek solutions to problems and your colleagues may be able to help. '*How many different types of writing can we get children to do using PenDown?*'; '*What ways are available to maximise the use of the computer in the Y4 classroom?*' In this case it may be appropriate to organise a brainstorming session as part of your day. It is harder than it might at first appear to make this technique work effectively and it might well be sensible to have some prepared answers as a reserve.

- Group work
  Nothing annoys INSET participants more than after a few brief moments of introduction to be told, '*Now go into groups and discuss . . .*' You need not only to be clear about why you want groups to talk together, and what will emerge from the discussions but, just as importantly, you will need to transmit this clearly to the participants. How long will they have, will they report back to the whole staff, will their conclusions be presented on an OHP? Remember to comment upon their contributions, otherwise teachers will feel it has been a waste of time.
- Snowballing
  Some reluctant participants can be encouraged to join in by quiet discussion of a proposition with their neighbour. At the conclusion this pair are then joined together with a similar couple and each explains their ideas to the other pair. The discussion gradually widens until a conclusion is reached which, hopefully, more represents the general opinion of the whole group rather than just the vocal minority. This is called snowballing.
- Plenary sessions at the end of each main block of time
  This gives you the chance to draw the various strands together and to tell participants what to expect after the break. It is also an opportunity to steer any group which has not stuck to their brief onto the main track again.
- Flexibility
  Your planning may include some options both in content and time allocated to various activities.
- Visits to part of the school, such as your software resource base.
- Time to consider management in the classroom
  A point in the day when teachers' professional expertise can be shared may be of particular help to younger/less experienced staff; and
- The needs of teachers of early years and those who work with older children.

If you are well prepared you will not be dashing around five minutes before you start. This is a useful time to chat and gauge the mood of the group. Try to move to some sort of simple opening activity fairly quickly. '*I'd like you to spend five*

Suggestion

Topics for discussion during in-service training might include

The teacher
What ICT skills are needed by the teacher to carry out the activity? What resources are required? What preparation would be needed?

minutes listing all the ICT activities which go on in your room. I will then ask one or two people to read out part of their list. Which of these ideas could be applied in your classroom?'

Participate yourself throughout the day, moving between groups. Try to avoid being didactic. Be prepared to summarise OFSTED, QCA, BECTA and LEA documents. During small group discussions take two minutes to check your plans and that you have the next step at your fingertips.

Don't rely on technology, videos etc. Used carefully they can help enormously, but can easily be overused and have even been known to break down! If you are using an OHP do not read out every word which appears on each slide. Either use the OHP to illustrate what you are saying or say things which amplify the ideas projected onto the screen. Avoid long periods of talk in the afternoon, especially the 'graveyard' slot immediately after lunch. It may be useful to finish off with the formulation of an action plan.

Professional development days can create an enormous momentum in the school. These events always need following up. They are never an end in themselves. Time is a precious commodity so it is essential that the day is viewed as a success and that there is a positive outcome with realistic, achievable targets. This will help to give everyone the feeling that their time on the day did lead to something useful. This will make it easier when eventually you want to repeat the process. The best way to facilitate future change is to provide for positive experience of change. (cf. Suggest topics in left-hand column)

Suggestion

Topics for discussion during in-service training might include

The curriculum
Where would the activity fit into the curriculum? How would it increase subject knowledge, skills and understanding? What ICT skills would the pupils acquire? Will all pupils take part in the activity? How will you cater for pupils of differing needs and abilities?

Sharing the load

Research has shown that computer disappointment occurs for one or more of four reasons:

trying to use the computer to solve the wrong problems;
lack of top management support;
poor user involvement; and,
inadequate attention to problems of human organisation.

To avoid as many as possible of these, coordinators need to promote the concept that ICT is a shared responsibility between different stakeholders. The relationship between the head and yourself in particular will be a major determinant in the establishment of a secure place for information and communications technology in your school. Secondary phase research undertaken by Owen (1992) showed that the key to computer success in the school was the strong leadership from senior management in favour of the use of computers and where they were used ineffectively it was mostly due to an abdication of responsibility by senior management.

The head teacher, along with governors will need to:
- encourage a sense of shared responsibility for ICT;
- encourage the development of links with other schools;
- exhibit a positive attitude towards ICT.

The IT coordinator should:
- promote the integration of ICT with all appropriate aspects of teaching and learning;
- act as a link with outside agencies;
- support and encourage colleagues;
- manage the provision and deployment of ICT resources;
- provide the first line of technical support; and,
- coordinate the review and evaluation of ICT policy.

Other subject coordinators should:
- consider the ways that ICT should be used in their own subjects.

All class teachers should:
- include planning for ICT in their forecasts;
- maximise the use of resources;
- assist the coordinator in the monitoring of pupil progress in ICT;
- share success and failure in order to support colleagues in ICT.

(after Underwood, 1996)

There are many ways in which the head teacher can give his or her support.

- the head teacher is seen to use ICT in running the school and thereby acts as a role model. This can be done by the use of ICT such as a laptop computer or a desk computer in the head's office; letters to parents being word processed and a spreadsheet conspicuously used to keep track of the school's day-to-day budget.
- ICT is given a high status in the school by the head who plays an important role in highlighting its importance.

- The IT coordinator needs to have easy access to this person and to be seen to have this access.
- There is a substantial budget available for the development of learning strategies by using ICT. This budget should be ring-fenced and subject to separate bid procedures. Other coordinators need to see that there will be a clear advantage to them in bidding for some of these resources.
- Inset funds are allocated to provide ICT training for staff.
- ICT is supported through the timetable.

(Based on Donnelly 1995)

Try to get such a set of responsibilities written into your school policy (see Chapter 9).

Evaluate what you have done

NCET and NAACE (the National Association of Advisers for Computers in Education) have produced a pack to support the inspection of IT in schools. It will be useful for coordinators to study this material in order to begin to develop an understanding of how to look at their own school through fresh eyes. For example, the quality of the management and administration of ICT is amplified thus:

Where IT is well managed, there will be a whole-school policy which details practice and informs decisions, the policy will have been developed with the involvement of all staff and will have the support of governors. It will deal with a range of issues from curriculum delivery to asset management. Operation of the policy will be regularly monitored and the policy itself periodically reviewed. The school will have a negotiated plan for the development of IT embracing both extension of its use and consequent requirements for staff training, resources and accommodation.

Where IT is not well managed, staff will be unclear about their contribution to the development of children's IT capability. Equipment remains unserviceable for long periods. Purchasing decisions are taken independently or on the spur of the moment, and lead to hardware or software environment which lacks coherence with both itself and the curriculum. Negative attitudes will be prevalent amongst the staff.

You can begin to evaluate your effectiveness as coordinator through comparison with such criteria. However, evaluation has to be an ongoing process, rather than something which we do later to determine our level of success. Evaluation needs to be inherent in the process rather than merely a step in the management plan. Periodic reviews where we assess, evaluate, refocus and re-emphasise are part of that process but not the whole story. Be sure to be seen to act on the result of the evaluation. Teachers will value the process if it leads to something but are naturally wary of anything which seems like time wasting.

There are a number of pre-requisites for evaluation. It is essential that both you and your colleagues are clear about your aims. Joseph Novak and Bob Gowin in *Learning How to Learn* (1984) remind us that in order to evaluate, we must first know what we mean by **value**. What positive outcomes did we seek to achieve? You will be better able to assess this if your school has a clear overall statement of purpose such as a mission statement or published aims. In turn, the aims relating to your subject area will correlate with those of your school as a whole and will thereby be the more easily understood.

Approaches to evaluation

How do you do it? David Playfoot et al. in *The Primary School Management Book* (1989) identify seven approaches:

1 structured staff discussion;
2 staff interviews;
3 work shadowing;
4 paired observation;
5 interest group sessions;
6 snowball sessions;
7 formulation of performance indicators.

The following strategies will assist the smooth running of any evaluation:

- Question your evaluation
  Why, when and what do you wish to evaluate? Who do you want to be involved?

- Feedback
  Be clear about the form of feedback from evaluation. It must be accurate and fairly stated so that staff can determine action to be taken.
- Realism
  Be realistic and honest at all times. It is worth waiting a little longer in order to carry the whole team with you. Do not attempt to force issues, overstate your case, or allow your enthusiasm to cause you to mislead your colleagues.
- Balance
  Seek a balanced picture where you can identify both positive and negative effects and where success and degrees of success (the word failure can usually be avoided!) can be reported.
- Progressively focus your attention
  As change takes time, so the context will alter. Some staff will be promoted and others will retire, new teachers will arrive; roles, responsibilities and priorities will change and government initiatives will come and then be superseded. Don't allow yourself to become frustrated by the fact that your targets do not stand still. Expect redefinition of your goals, plan for the possibility of new initiatives and where possible use them to your advantage.
- Use a mix of strategies and approaches
  No one method alone will do. Variety will allow everyone to contribute the more fully.
- Manage the evaluation
  Sensitivity is required. Your management of the evaluation process should be deliberate. You must seek meaningful and worthwhile evaluation but always recognise that the school is run by human beings with frailties and the capacity to misjudge situations, just like we do!

(after Cross and Harrison, 1994)

You might wish to simply take O'Neill's (1996) basic test of the value of the work of the curriculum coordinator, which is the extent to which it helps:

overcome the normal working isolation of classroom teachers;
enhance collaborative curriculum development within the school; and crucially,
improve the quality of teaching and learning. (p. 26)

Conclusion

A successful team needs people with skills, knowledge, aptitudes, interests and personalities which interlock in order to make a workable organisation. The nature of your context may or may not lend itself to this ideal. However, you have to work with all of them and appreciate that however enthusiastic you are about your proposals, coordination like politics, is merely the art of the possible.

Part two

What IT coordinators need to know

Chapter 4

What IT coordinators need to know about children and computers

ICT's potential

 *IT offers potential for effective group working.*

Erault and Hoyles (1989); Light (1993); Messer and Light (1991) in NCET (1993)

'One of the most impressive aspects of the use of the computer in the primary classroom is the amount of talk which is generated' (Straker and Govier, 1996, p. 128) The type and quality of talk is of course dependent upon the software being used and the degree of teacher intervention, but the focus provided for speaking and listening, reflection and participation, is of use to native English speakers and for those children to whom English is a second language.

The computer is a powerful and highly motivating learning tool. Used creatively it can enhance our primary pupils' repertoire of learning skills; increase their access to the curriculum especially for those children with a variety of individual needs and from diverse cultural heritages. In primary schools its effective use also poses issues of classroom management, which in their solution can force teachers to confront many of the challenges of today. It has for example been argued elsewhere (Harrison, 1994c) that facilitating group work can help schools:

- to value what children bring to school and explicitly, their cultural diversity;

- to encourage children to value themselves as part of human kind, which celebrates both similarities and differences;
- to allow children the opportunity to stand back and view situations objectively;
- to allow children to express what they honestly feel about themselves, the treatment of themselves and others and their everyday conflict situations;
- to prepare all pupils for life in a pluralistic society characterised by differentiation in language, ethnicity and/or cultural heritage;
- to encourage children to look for strategies for resolving problems, especially conflicts and to capitalise on cooperative communalities;
- to help children to discover aspects of their own culture, particularly those which help them to locate themselves;
- to foster empathy by imagining the feelings of people both in similar and different situations to their own;
- to use everyday situations to discuss uses and abuses of power and to consider individual and collective rights and responsibilities.

With increasing pressure on schools to demonstrate the rise in children's attainment in academic subjects, there can be a tendency for such important goals to become sidelined. Opportunities can be created to explore these issues, on the way to achievements in many subject areas, by using computers as a tool. The collaborative use of a highly motivational tool such as a computer provides us with a means to facilitate children's growth in these areas. For 'group work around a computer may be more genuinely collaborative than other group work, thereby enabling more focused group talk' (Davis, Desforges, Jessel, Somekh, Taylor and Vaughan, 1992, p. 20).

There are many who argue of course that a computer 'is more than a tool because it embodies . . . the capacity to interact with us as a surrogate of its human programmers.' (Somekh and Davies, 1991). Nonetheless it may be easier for coordinators to present to teachers the metaphor of using computers as a tool, to move the school toward achieving collaborative ventures rather than to fathom the mind of the software engineer.

After all a **tool** can be used:

- to unlock hidden issues in a number of different ways for different purposes;
- to prise open feelings;
- to empower the tool user; and,
- to help build ideas about teaching for equality in gender, race, and disability.

The computer is a many-headed tool. In using a computer to produce a class magazine, for example, technology, art and English are all brought together. Data from surveys and numerical information can be accommodated and in the act of editing such an item, cross-curricular themes and dimensions will need to be debated and considered. The editorial team will need to find ways of working together and adhere to agreed principles and styles of presentation.

The computer, allied to communications technology can be a window on the world. Websites and classrooms from many thousands of miles away can be downloaded in a matter of seconds. Children can visit the jungles of Malaysia and the Rocky mountains and what's more talk with other children who live there. Hence another form of group work is possible and a real contribution to spiritual and moral development.

In a 1993 survey IT coordinators were asked by the author about the use to which their class computer was being put at one specified time in a week in January (Harrison, 1994). The most striking feature of the results is that 29 per cent of all the available computers were not being used at all at the time of the snapshot. This was in replies by the most interested schools in the district (some 27 per cent replied to the questionnaire). We can safely assume that in those schools that did not reply the percentage being used was not greater.

This is an important finding in that, for many children whose lives will increasingly be dominated by computer technology, their only experience with IT is in the classroom. If they don't get experience there they get it nowhere. The use of computers to support curricular goals is clearly established in almost all primary schools. In addition it is argued here that tasks can be presented in such a way that children can be stimulated to express ideas and concern, seek information to counter argument and debate, establish environments and reflect on situations. However, despite heavy capital investment by LEAs, PTAs and other sources many children are still not getting that entitlement. OFSTED reports repeatedly refer to the low level of use of the school's computers as a major factor in holding back children's progress.

A further survey in three primary schools in the same LEA carried out by the author in December 1992, asked boys and girls in junior classes if they had a computer of their own at home, or access to one owned by another member of the family. The claimed ownership of computers was 58 per cent, 40 per cent and 38 per cent respectively. When the survey was analysed by sex some interesting results were noted. (Harrison, 1994)

Bias in attitudes between the sexes toward computers is consistently reported in the literature. Professor Celia Hoyles comments

> *It is, therefore, difficult to avoid the disturbing conclusion that girls are learning less than boys about computers and therefore acquiring less understanding as to how they might use computers for their own purposes* (Hoyles, 1988)

She found a consistent difference in attitude and access to IT between the sexes especially at older ages. In this survey this appears not to be the case in two of the junior aged populations but is markedly so in one school with a high ethnic minority intake.

In order to see if family structure and shared ownership would affect this picture the data was further analysed. Children were asked how many brothers and sisters they had living at home with them and later, in a separate section, whether there was a computer in the house that they could use. Replies were then looked for where boys had no sisters and girls no brothers. It was difficult to generalise from such a sample but this research does relate to that of Smithers and Zientek (1991) who found that gender stereotyping was much higher in Asian groups and amongst those with brothers and sisters than for the population at large. Thus especially for ethnic minority girls, the experiences which they have with computers in primary classrooms is therefore vital.

By the year 2000 more than two-thirds of all jobs in Europe will need IT skills and over the next decade over 90 per cent of the growth in the UK will come from women entering and re-entering the workforce. Currently only 22 per cent of IT professionals and 4 per cent of IT managers are females. (NCET, TV 1996 Award winning video: *Why me why IT?*) In the recent government white paper *Realising our Potential*: put together as a strategy for science, engineering and technology, the authors acknowledge that women are the country's biggest single most undervalued and therefore unused human resource. Factors contributing to this include lack of access to role models, lack of awareness on the part of careers advisers and teachers, inflexible employers, poor recruitment practices, lack of parental and social encouragement, inadequate training, timing of schools' option choices and aggressive computer games.

As coordinator you could be a real influence in the move to reverse this trend. In your colleagues' classrooms do boys take the active roles and do teachers allow the girls to just watch? Why not encourage peer tutoring and get girls to learn some applications first and subsequently pass their skills and understanding on to the boys?

ICT and curriculum development

The influence of ICT is wider than just supporting aspects of various programmes of study, or debating the best way to use software. Computers can alter the way curriculum content is organised but, as yet, in many schools consideration of such curriculum development is some way off. We may consider advantages of such innovation as:

- Work with computers can provide a focus for colleagues to develop a commonly understood policy about the grouping of children including those from diverse cultural backgrounds, for certain tasks.

- Providing a knowledge of applications and technical support can encourage confidence and self-esteem in the provider. To whom should such responsibility be given? Can such responsibility be shared to show the value given to skills, knowledge and experience of different children? Can the enhancement of self-esteem be a criteria in choices made?
- Establishing an overview of the use of computers throughout the school can highlight their importance in acting as a tool for expression and communication and give opportunities to demonstrate the respect given by the school to children's mastery of their mother tongue.
- Helping teachers to see where work in ICT can support teaching and learning, can re-emphasise the need for meeting individual needs.
- Organising resources so that they are physically accessible, forces consideration of the intellectual, cultural and language accessibility of material.

Some responses to the challenges outlined above include the following:

- The 'twinning' of schools can be enhanced by the use of electronic mail that can set up a dialogue between children from different areas;
- the grouping of children chosen to use the computer may be used as a tool of social engineering, involving 'isolates' and getting children to mix;
- using LOGO children learn to break a problem down into smaller elements and solve them independently;
- the issues exposed when software is selected and evaluated may become a growth point for discussion between staff about classroom purposes and practices.

For example, Meadows's (1992) report on the electronic mail project, *EMTENET*, which linked students from a variety of countries and cultures, showed a personal element for many ethnic minority students taking part.

> *Telecommunications allows direct links between . . . school pupils, without the barriers of (possibly out of date) text books or someone else's views coming between the participants.*

An American initiative used electronic conferencing of a more structured kind to provide prospective teachers with opportunities to become aware of their own taken-for-granted assumptions, acknowledge the validity in perspectives different from their own and reflect upon the choices they make (Harrington, 1992). Developments for pupils may follow.

Empowerment is implied here. If 'the purpose of education is liberation . . . not the development of objects' (President Nyerere's 1974 speech quoted in Shan and Bailey, 1991) then it is ironic that the most technical of subjects ICT may take us nearer to that ideal.

Effective use of ICT in primary school

The school's published output will also be enhanced by good quality word processing and printing and as coordinator you may well enhance your profile if you can help the school to achieve improvements to their published output. A school brochure is most useful, especially one which demonstrates the celebration of pupils' various achievements and publicly acknowledges the diversity of its pupils. The inclusion of stories and other computer work produced by pupils will enhance the school's reputation within the wider community and enhance the self-image of children whose work is selected.

Records of achievement, in which pupils can display what they know, understand and can do, can have real effects on the self-esteem and sense of self-worth of pupils. Make sure that the reproduction is the best you can possibly manage (use the school's computer and tell readers that you have done so). With cheap hand-held scanners becoming increasingly more available, schools will be able to create computer images of photographs and art work done in school to place within their documents.

Arranging for groups of children to carry out a complex task in which they need to cooperate is very demanding. Teachers often complain that, with their limited share of computer time, it takes half a term to get anything done. There are plenty of times, however, when one or two children could be finishing off the analysis of a database or putting finishing touches to a newsletter outside lesson times. Some children love staying in at playtime during cold weather and using the computer can provide a useful occupation.

Flexible planning

Careful planning can allow groups or individuals to use the machine at times when they are not involved with the rest of the class.

- During assembly times
- At playtime and lunch hour
- After school and before school starts
- During registration, story time and while the class are doing PE
- Those not going swimming could use the machine at this time

This will often prompt the use of temporary flexible groupings which can help breakdown some of the more fixed groups which can dominate the organisation of such work in primary classrooms. Labelling children according to perceived ability and grouped permanently according to that perception is countered by this measure.

Although much primary school work is characterised as groups of children working together the reality has often been described as a collective monologue. Often there is no evidence of either cooperation nor collaborative learning.

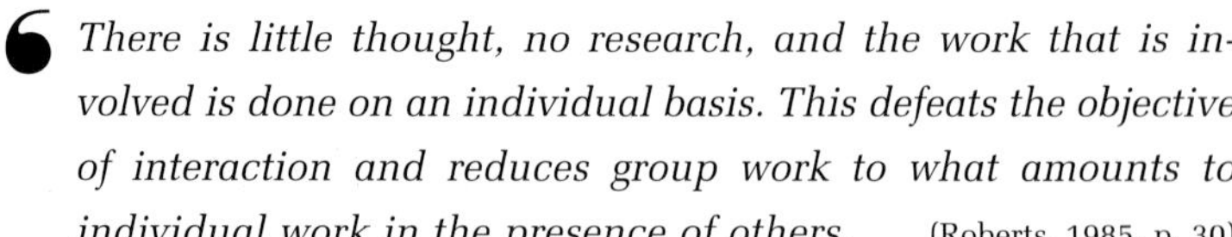

> *There is little thought, no research, and the work that is involved is done on an individual basis. This defeats the objective of interaction and reduces group work to what amounts to individual work in the presence of others.* (Roberts, 1985, p. 30)

It is only by producing the conditions of small group work that concepts skills and attitudes, such as cooperation, conflict, power and inequality, similarity and differences and rational argument can be developed.

Working in flexible groups, exploring and valuing the contributions of others is excellent preparation for life in a complex and culturally diverse society. It has a real role in fulfilling Verma's (1993b) third function of education '(it) sets the patterns and models of behaviour which young people are expected to manifest in group settings in the school, in the world of work and ultimately in the wider social setting'.

Small group work can lead to:

- a secure environment that some less confident pupils need in order to express their ideas;
- some children accepting responsibility to help others;
- full involvement of all the children in the task;
- children recognising the contributions of others to be as important as their own; and,
- children being able to recognise the individuality of others thus breaking down the stereotypes and prejudices often associated with inequality.

(based upon ideas in 'Working toward social justice' in *A Spanner in the Works* by Brown, Barnfield and Stone, 1990.)

Working with LOGO has been seen to be one of the best ways in which children can be encouraged to work cooperatively on a problem-solving task. They have no choice but to pool ideas, listen to each other and try out a variety of solutions. This checklist might be used by coordinators to help teachers to consider whether the use of LOGO will achieve their ends. The chart shown in Figure 4.1 may prove useful.

The consequences of other aspects of work with ICT also coincide with this agenda. For example by offering children the chance to interrogate, order and present data teachers can equip children to understand their most valuable lesson namely that 'Facts are always impregnated with interpretations, and although some are more plausible than others, all interpretations are partial' (Verma, 1993).

To achieve our social goals we need to put children into situations where they share and discuss ideas, compromise to gain agreements, achieve success and to do this in a safe environment. The overall lesson to be learned from many school and classroom projects is that you have to get close to children to get them to open up and willingly explore their own feelings and prejudices. Gaine (1987) talks of the 'Grange Hill phenomenon':

A self help checklist — cooperative work and LOGO across the school		
Question	Your response	Action
■ What aspects of co-operative work do I want to encourage teachers to plan?		
■ Where does ICT enhance this aspect of the curriculum?		
■ How familiar are the children with LOGO?		
■ How do I want teachers to group the children?		
■ How familiar are the children in many classes with the problem solving concepts to be presented to them?		
■ Do teachers understand the application themselves?		
■ What other curriculum areas are being experienced at the same time?		
■ How will teachers carry out any assessment associated with the task?		
■ What evidence of pupil progress will they need to collect?		
■ What will I regard as successful activities?		

FIG 4.1
Using LOGO to promote cooperative work

school is the backdrop against which (children) act out the important things in their lives . . . friendships/group values. . . .' The important things happen between lessons in Grange Hill (and in real schools). Teachers are seldom privy to this world

(Gaine, 1987)

Small groups working on computers give a context within which teachers can get closer. Furthermore learning by trial and error, always an aim in primary classrooms, can be a risky business in real life. A micro-world can provide teachers with an opportunity otherwise denied. For pupils, ICT can become an empowering equal opportunity experience with potential for fostering cultural cohesion. ICT is a tool. How it is used, on what content and to what ends its use is directed, are of essence in a diverse society.

Group work around a programmable toy, such as Roamer also has implications for children's social development. Successful task completion involves cooperation, sharing and discussing ideas and a sense of vision.

Personal attributes

Learning with a computer, like other kinds of learning, provides many opportunities for children to work together in a group. Collaborative work should enable children to take part in collective decision making, to listen to other people's comments and to have respect for each person's contributions to the work of the group.

Children have different approaches to the use of computers. The inter-personal skills which children develop are not unique to the work they undertake on the computer but such small group work may be effective in allowing personal development alongside any other learning that takes place.

It is vital that all children develop positive attitudes towards using the computer and that girls as well as boys feel confident about using the machine. Learning skills which may be developed through ICT include: research skills; development of personal confidence; cooperation by teaching each other; learning from feedback; observing patterns and justifying generalisations, and seeing connections.

For computer work to be successful children need to feel responsible for the equipment and the software. They also need encouragement to be systematic when they work — to keep orderly notes and to present their work well. They need to save work on their own disc or in their own directory on a hard disc. They need to respect the work of others learning what is public and what is private property.

These are transferrable skills and attitudes — and ones your teacher colleagues will want to encourage.

Chapter 5

What IT coordinators need to know about using computers across the curriculum

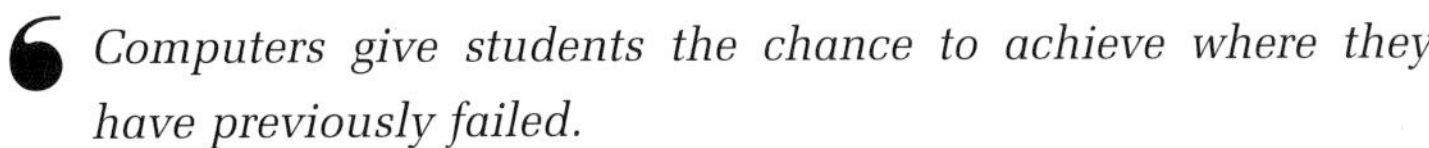

Computers give students the chance to achieve where they have previously failed.

Howard (1993); Daiute (1992) in NCET (1993)

As you develop ICT throughout the school you will increasingly feel the need to equip yourself with relevant knowledge and skills in order to give your colleagues support. This will involve you becoming increasingly credible as a consultant, improving your own teaching, inter-personal and presentation skills, acquiring knowledge and demonstrating positive attitudes towards teaching and learning with ICT in all subjects of the curriculum.

Working through the coordinators of other subjects

Some IT coordinators may find that there are only limited opportunities to influence colleagues though in-service days and ICT cannot always be a high priority on the School Development Plan (SDP). The lesson many IT coordinators have had to learn is that working through other subject coordinators, persuading them that using ICT will enhance teaching and learning in their subject, can be an equally effective way to get the message across.

It may help to be reminded of some guidelines for effective communication quoted in Part 1. Teachers charged with the responsibility of promoting curricular areas to their colleagues may find an advantage in choosing an appropriate messenger. The status of the source of the information is often seen to indicate its importance. The following list is based on the principles in Dean's book *Managing the Primary School* (1987).

- Teachers are more likely to be responsive to the advice of coordinators if addressed personally rather than by memo. The coordinator you need on your side will be more likely to take home your message if you tell her so.
- Rousing the interest of the listener is necessary in order to get your message across. What are the present concerns of the targeted coordinator? Can you obtain on-approval software to meet that need? Can you be using it in your own room when she happens to pass?
- Information is more likely to be valued if it gives an advantage in power or status to the listener. If the coordinator is more likely to achieve her ambitions or complete the task she has been set, she will indeed take notice of you, and be a powerful force behind the changes you desire.
- No-one likes to be seen as letting down their team or working group. Can you publicly express backing for one or more of her initiatives creating a bond of support between you? She may then feel more committed to your joint initiative.
- The situation (surroundings, time of day etc.) should be chosen carefully in order to predispose the listener to be receptive. Tackling your targeted coordinator while she is on the way to the staff meeting is probably too late to influence her substantially.

Encouraging the use of ICT in mathematics

IT in the Mathematics National Curriculum Orders

Key Stage 1

Using and applying mathematics
Developing mathematics reasoning such as by asking questions including '*What would happen if?' and* '*Why?' — considering the behaviour of a programmable toy.*

Number
Pupils should be given opportunities to use computer software including database.

Shape, space and measure
Pupils should be given opportunities to:

use IT devices e.g. *programmable toys, turtle graphics packages.*

Understanding and using properties of position and movement
Understand angle as a measure of turn and recognise quarter-turns, e.g. giving instructions for rotating a programmable toy; recognise right angles.

Key Stage 2

Number
Pupils should be given opportunities to use calculators, computers and a range of other resources as tools for exploring number structure and to enable work with realistic data.

Shape, space and measure
Pupils should be given opportunities to use computers to create and transform shapes.

Handling data
Pupils should be given opportunities to:

use computers as a source of interesting data, and as a tool for representing data.

Collecting, representing and interpreting data:

collect and represent discrete data appropriately using graphs and diagrams, including block graphs, pictograms and line graphs; interpret a wider range of graphs and diagrams that represent data, including pie charts, using a computer where appropriate.

Using and applying mathematics
Communicating mathematically use mathematical forms of communication, including diagrams, tables, graphs and computer printouts.

The mathematics coordinators' job is nearly as difficult as yours! 'Mathematics is both difficult to teach and to learn' (Cockcroft, 1982) and the insecurity which many primary school teachers may feel can only be deepened by the periodic attacks on mathematics teaching mounted by the press. Yet successful mathematics teaching has to do with confidence.

Women sometimes hold the view that mathematics is a male domain, perhaps promoted by teachers' expectations that boys will find it easy while girls will be less likely to succeed. Other beliefs include that mathematics teaching places an emphasis on speed, with the associated false expectation that mathematicians find answers almost instantly; and still others have vivid memories of failure (Davies, 1990). Any help you can offer to build the confidence of staff in this area will most certainly be welcomed.

'*Fear of failing*' at mathematics is an attitude which prevails amongst many of the adult population including teachers. The approach adopted by teachers continues to have a profound effect upon pupils' attitudes to mathematics. Research shows that negative attitudes often persist into adulthood. Can the use of ICT to support teaching help to dispel this attitude?

Are the school's intentions in the use of ICT to support learning in mathematics made clear by the mathematics policy document? Does the coordinator know the range of the programs available? Do teachers know what mathematics software children have used previously when they receive a new class? Do parents know what you are trying to do when using computers to teach mathematics to children of different ages and abilities?

Teaching mathematics through the use of computers and other ICT devices and using mathematical ICT experiences to enhance children's competence and confidence in ICT are valid aspirations for both you and the mathematics coordinator. Why not join forces to achieve it?

Consider why we spend so much time teaching mathematics in primary schools. After language work, mathematics takes the lion's share of the timetable of all primary classes.

> *Mathematics is taught not only because it is useful but because it should be a source of delight and wonder, offering pupils intellectual excitement and an appreciation of its essential creativity.* (NCC Mathematics — Non-Statutory Guidance (NSG))

After all, mathematics is a powerful means of communication — to represent, to explain and to predict; an increasingly powerful tool in many commercial and industrial environments; a discipline which, with others, can contribute to the development of logical thinking skills; and also worthy of study for its intrinsic interest, beauty and enjoyment. These will be some of the starting points for the mathematics curriculum leader.

What ICT resources can you suggest to help teachers to teach mathematics?

Databases

Databases are frequently used to show both children and adults the power of the computer. The speed at which micros can make calculations, sort data, and the graphic capabilities employed to show the results are all impressive. Whichever package your school has got, you will be able to obtain specimen files. Encourage the mathematics coordinator to use these at home. Help her how to find out what analyses are possible; how to print out a list or a pie chart; to delete or replace a file; and to print out an individual record. Can she sort a subset of data (boys/British moths) only? Do the publishers suggest ways in which classes could use the program? The oft heard criticism of graph work in primary classrooms in the past has been the disproportionate amount of time children spend constructing the chart compared to the mathematical thought so prompted. The interpretation of pie charts and graphs has been said to be particularly poor. With the use of ICT that ratio can be reversed, as the time-consuming aspects of drawing graphs are simply and swiftly handled leaving pupils time to consider such matters as which is the best sort of graph to use; what will we expect; how shall we explain our results? Can you persuade the coordinator to promote the use of data handling programs to teachers?

Drill and practise

These programs are often scathingly attacked as the unacceptable face of computer use. You might argue however, that in mathematics as such programs often support specific learning objectives, they generally give instant reward, they have appeal to some pupils, the work can allow for differentiation (the rest of the class being occupied with other matters) and spread the practise of certain skills across a number of media. Such software is occasionally used as an electronic blackboard demonstrating a method to obtain the right answer in an attractive and often tuneful manner. The question you and the maths curriculum leader will need to answer is whether this is the best use of an expensive and scarce resource.

As Judith Judd (1991) points out in *Children, Computers and the National Curriculum,*

> *It is more important for children to become skilled in general purpose computer applications than to spend time practising spelling tests. Skilled exploitation of a spreadsheet, graphics package or desktop publishing programme . . . can improve personal productivity dramatically and is also transferable between topics . . .* (Judd, 1991)

A variation of this is the use of software to create a series of unique drill and practise work cards tailored to stress specific number bonds, number sequences, operations or combinations of these. Such a programme for the A3000 series is **Maths Card** which many teachers would view as a boon for computation work as it does not occupy the computer for more than the time it takes for the teacher to set up the parameters and print out the result, leaving the machine itself for more creative work. A downloadable alternative is available from the Argosphere Internet Web site. You could work with the mathematics coordinator to develop a series of exemplar files as a start for teachers to develop their own work to match the needs of their classes.

It could be that some teachers may need to be persuaded to use the computer in ways which extend children's skills in using their imaginations by composing written texts, creating graphics, generating and solving problems, devising programs and investigating data. Those of us who react negatively to the idea that children can be taught by computers are more enthusiastic about the concept of children themselves teaching computers routines and procedures. This is the concept behind LOGO.

LOGO and turtle graphics

LOGO and turtle graphics are widely appreciated as important elements in work in ICT in primary classrooms. Many references to such work are contained in the National Curriculum (mathematics, technology, science) and teachers who have worked with children in this area report enthusiastically on the benefits for children both in their development of cognition, their confidence and, by the mode of working, their ability to cooperate in problem solving situations.

In her acclaimed book *Children and Computers*, Anita Straker points out that there are three related but different aspects of the use of LOGO with young children that make it worthwhile:

- it can encourage discovery learning;
- it can help children to develop mathematical concepts;
- it can provide insight into the power of programming.

Some mathematics coordinators will consider this work better undertaken with a programmable robot such as *PIP*, *Pixie* or *Roamer* and you may wish to consider the purchase of such items to add to the stock of equipment under your control, or better still get it bought through the mathematics curriculum budget.

Islamic geometry and Vedic maths have been brought together in Bunyard and Brine's LOGO programme (Straker, 1989) (available on Micromath Disc 3). This helps to introduce children to exquisite spirolateral patterns drawn quickly and easily by means of the computer. Teachers would do well to remind children that such designs were, and still are, created using only a ruler, compass and protractor (Shan and Bailey, 1991).

By working with the mathematics coordinator, knowing the equipment, software and needs of the mathematics scheme you might be able to develop a table of help for the mutual benefit of children's learning in both areas. Below are some of the areas which may be of interest to the mathematics coordinator.

Statements largely from the Programmes of Study for MATHEMATICS	Uses of ICT based on your school's equipment, software and peripherals — work this out with the coordinator — some suggestions
Developing mathematical language in number; the properties and movement of shapes, measures.	Working with drawing packages to explore symmetry, reflection and relationships. Using ICT to develop mathematical language and forms of communication
Understand bigger than, next to, before. Use programmable toys and turtle graphics packages and grow to understand the relationships between number, size and distance.	Mega math project web site brings unusual and important ideas to elementary school classrooms http://www.c3.lanl.gov/mega-math Roamer, PIP, Pixie, floor turtles.
Developing reasoning, sorting, classifying, making comparisons and searching for patterns	Working with programs designed to foster problem solving abilities which encourage children to ask questions and devise alternatives. Using LOGO to support problem solving skills and extend children's mathematical thinking Working with ready made databases and sorting, branching data programs to represent data by a wide range of graphs and diagrams Use My World 2, sorting and grading screens.
Collect and represent data appropriately using graphs and diagrams, including block graphs, pictograms and line graphs; interpret as a wider range of graphs and diagrams that represent data including pie charts using a computer where appropriate. Interpret tables used in everyday life. Understand and use measures of average, leading towards the mode, the median and mean relevant contexts, and the range as a measure of spread.	Working with ready made databases to represent data by a wide range of graphs and diagrams Adventure games and associated mathematical challenges Handling Data — use computers both as a source of interesting data, and as a tool for representing data. Electronic information charts (such as British Rail timetables) Real data from Internet / cross curricular sources Databases and spreadsheets such as Junior Pinpoint* (see example) picturepoint, pictogram (Acorn) and counting pictures (PC) older children use First Workshop (PC)
Recognise and use geometrical features of shapes including vertices, sides, edges, surfaces, rectangles, circles, squares, triangles, cubes, cuboids, hexagons, pentagons, cylinders, spheres — recognise reflective symmetry, translations, rotations, recognise right angles	Spreadsheets for recording Some CD ROM products A gallery of on-line interactive geometry Web site http://www.geom.umn.edu/apps/gallery.html Drawing programs where sections of designs can be relocated, rotated and copied.
Consider a range of patterns including some drawn from different cultural traditions	Drawing programs LOGO and Vedic geometry
Work with simple probability. Use evens, fair, unfair, certain, likely, probably.	Some adventure games LOGO using the RANDOM (x) variable
Investigate number. Use some properties of numbers including multiples, factors, squares, extending to primes, cubes and square roots. Relationships including multiple of, factor of and symmetrical to.	Shell Centre for Mathematical Education http://acorn.edu.nottingham.ac.uk/shellCent/ Real data such as that from the Commonwealth of Learning, a Canadian web site with files of facts, figures and statistics http://www.col.org/ Purpose-made programs such as animated number and Fun School — under 5 The World of Number interactive multi-media package
Know number bonds and times tables facts. Understand and use in context fractions and percentages to estimate, compare and describe proportions of as a whole	Learning multiplication tables http://www.bbc.co.uk/education/megamaths Purpose made programs Use real data derived from CD ROM encyclopaedia More mathematics web sites are listed in part 5.

FIG 5.1
ICT and the mathematics curriculum

*Junior Pinpoint allows children to show the same information in a variety of ways: frequency of eye colour

All answer sheets

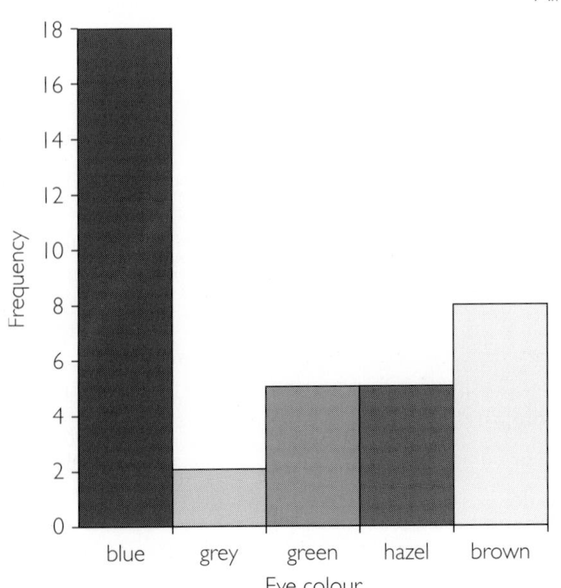

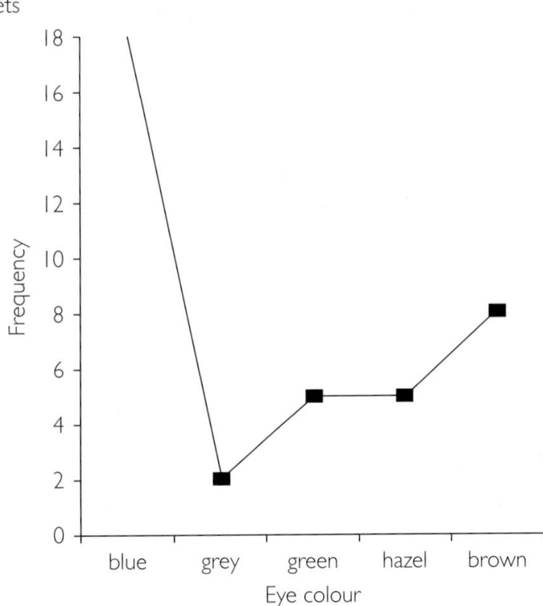

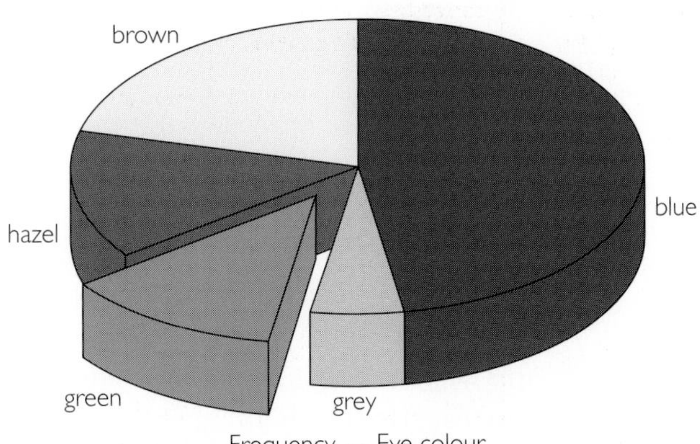

Frequency — Eye colour

English

IT in the English National Curriculum Orders

Key Stage 1

Reading
Pupils should be introduced to and should read information, both in print and on screen. They should be encouraged to make use of a range of sources of information, including dictionaries, IT based reference materials, encyclopaedias and information presented in fictional form.

Writing
Pupils should have opportunities to plan and review their writing, assembling and developing their ideas on paper and on screen.

Key Stage 2

Reading
Range:
Pupils should read and use a wide range of sources of information, including those not designed for children. The range of non-fiction should include IT-based reference materials.

Key Skills:
Pupils should be given opportunities to plan, draft and improve their own work on paper and on screen.

The wide range of responsibilities assigned to the English coordinator probably means that she will appreciate any help you can offer to improve teaching and learning in speaking and listening, reading and children's writing. The general character of speaking in groups around the computer is highlighted in the previous chapter and key elements from this section might be usefully brought to her attention. ICT can also assist in helping children to master the basic skills in reading, recognising letters, word families, associating sounds with text and with the range of talking books available this has been made easier.

Word processing

World processing is recognised as the most popular single use of computers in primary schools and may be a good focus for collaboration between yourself and the English coordinator. The use of a word processor can help children to become familiar with the keyboard in the initial phase. It removes the need for simultaneous concentration on all the aspects of production and encourages drafting, checking for errors, editing and collaborative writing in later stages.

> *For some a change in the way text is presented increases its value and provides some 'mental distance' from its production both of which encourage re-writing.*
>
> (Davis, Desforge, Jessel, Somekh, Taylor and Vaughan, 1992)

It may help us to convince children to view writing as a culturally mutable entity. In modern 32 bit computers (such as the A3000), fonts in a variety of languages are available and Punjabi and Urdu versions of *Folio* are produced for the BBC range of computers. *Full Phases* and PenDown have a speech option whereby text can be spoken as words are typed in. Cloze procedures can be generated by using children's own writing and word banks are provided to give younger children their first experience of using a thesaurus.

The use of different fonts and borders stimulates a sense of audience and the final product can usually be produced in a number of formats (large for the wall display, medium-size to accompany a picture, smaller for an entry in a newspaper or collection of works).

A point of collaboration between the IT and English coordinators is the need to consider whether a variety of word processors with different facilities are needed to help children to write for various audiences and exploit any cultural diversity amongst pupils. For example different children may want to write:

- newspaper reports about events in different countries;
- an obituary;
- a play script for a puppet show;
- the musings of a famous person;
- a child's record of achievement in mother tongue;
- evidence from a trial;
- the recipe;

- an advertisement for the newspaper;
- an account of using chopsticks for the first time;
- the tale of Rama and Sita;
- about a holiday;
- a script for an assembly;
- instructions or directions;
- a seventeenth century version of a modern tale;
- a message in a bottle;
- a doctor's report;
- a poster in two different languages;
- a letter/postcard to a friend;
- a job application;
- a letter of complaint;
- a conversation.

They might find using only one type of word processor quite limiting. Can expression be encouraged by providing children with the option of a variety of packages? What progression does the English coordinator expect and how can this be assisted by different software?

Collaborative writing can also be promoted by the use of word processing. One class of 11 year olds, where the teacher wanted to encourage the children to discuss their feelings about themselves, the people around them and the outside world in order to begin highlighting similarities, differences and injustices, the teacher started by getting children to brainstorm 'feeling' words. Typed onto a computer, the list could have been saved each day and, when reloaded, appear on the screen for all to view. Using these words groups of children wrote about such situations as:

- how they felt when someone pushed them;
- how they felt if a friend was ill;
- how they felt in the dark.

Later children were asked to work in groups and define 'feelings':

> *'Feelings are something inside you and sometimes hurt'*
> *'Feelings are thoughts. Feelings are things inside you. Things*

> *in your brain. They can drive you crazy. They can drive you into dangerous things.'*
>
> (Brown, Barnfield and Stone, 1990)

Collaborative word processing was examined by Jessel (1992). He suggests that less re-drafting takes place than may be usual because the child not only has to have thoughts, but be able to express a rationale for them and this might make intellectual demands which many 9 and 10 year olds may find difficult to meet. If this is so, it is even more imperative that such opportunities are provided because the intellectual challenge of working in such a way in a larger group, perhaps under the scrutiny of a teacher, is even more daunting.

Many word processing programs now allow a degree of Desk Top Publishing (even those which do not can be utilised in a DTP process, which also stands for Dab with Tippex and Photocopy). Clip-Art pictures can be sized, added to *Phases* and *PenDown* and positioned according to need. Scenes from a variety of stories, fables, festivals and cultural traditions will become more and more available as the demands continue to grow, and CD ROMS, which capture images from TV and film and translate them for use on the computer, become more common in primary schools.

Joy, Hartland and Tolley (1992) give a variety of ideas that the IT coordinator might use to help teachers to set varied and interesting tasks for pupils to enable them to:

- convery ideas to the screen where they can be read clearly;
- edit the text to correct spelling and punctuation;
- insert and delete words and phrases to enhance the text; move pieces of the text to another part of the work;
- save and retrieve the text so that it can be used over a period of time; and,
- print the result for a wider audience.

An alternative tried by many schools is the Email project, or pairing children from different schools as Key Pals. The problem many schools find with pairing is that after children

Areas of work from within the Programme of Study for ENGLISH	Uses of ICT based on your school's equipment, software and peripherals — work this out with the coordinator — some suggestions in *italics*
Speaking and listening	Reading talking books — talking word processors. Using a tape recorder to create a story book. Report on a radio or TV programme, describe a photograph.
Use of Standard English Considering how talk is influenced by the purpose and intended audience.	Working in groups with adults on solving problems in adventure programmes, using Roamers, taking turns in speaking to give instructions.
Words and their use and interpretation in different contexts.	Teachers' own word processed files using words with similar meanings, words associated with specific occasions, the characteristic language of story telling. Commercial word games.
Phonic knowledge	Reading talking books — talking word processors
Word recognition	Various games, CD ROMs
Graphic knowledge	
Reading different genre, challenging texts, with a variety of structural and organisational features.	CD ROMS of encyclopaedia, scientific or historical packages, newspapers. The Internet for example to Encyclopaedia Britannica on-line (partial access) http:///www.eb.com/ Inference and deduction from text-based adventure games.
Plan, draft, revise, proof read, present	Word processing leads to rapid and painless re-drafting. Use of different fonts, thesauruses, spell checker.
Developing writing composition skills, presentational skills, a widening appreciation of a variety of forms of writing for different purposes and becoming aware of how an audience receives the work	At Key Stage 2 pupils should be taught the features of presentation and layout by using word processors with various levels of sophistication. Use of web sites such as the Daily Telegraph, Walt Disney and on-line owl writing lab* (see example) http://www.telegraph.co.uk/ http://www.nwnet/ v brandon/stories/ http://www.eduweb.co.uk/index.html/ Kids Chat is at http://www.sutton.lincs/sch.uk/index.htm
Spelling	Word attack programmes, talking word processors such as Clicker plus, talking Pendown, Wordshark, Startwrite.

FIG 5.2
ICT and the English curriculum

have told each other of their favourite crisp flavour and their pets, the conversation dries up. Email projects — set up by teachers from different schools (to write a joint comic or newspaper reflecting two localities, for example) — are more successful. Kids chat pages are also used to stimulate real writing.

Here are some of the concerns of English coordinators. Can you work with them to see if the use of ICT can enhance children's experiences? (Figure 5.2)

Thomas the Clown http://www.logo.com/catalogue/titles/thomas/thomas1.html

Thomas the Clown

Slide Show

Price/Order

New search

Home

Funny Faces

Help Thomas build a picture of a clown's face by choosing the correct face parts. When the puzzles get harder, how good are you at spotting the order in which the face parts need to be picked to build exactly the right expression?

(Reproduced with permission. Logotron can be seen in an online catalogue at www.logo.com)

Science

IT in the Science National Curriculum Orders

Key Stage 1 and 2

Systematic enquiry
use IT to collect, store, retrieve and present scientific information.

The science coordinator should be a close ally as so many features of their work coincide with yours. Just as with computers, many teachers were until recently unfamiliar with many scientific concepts. Experimentation which is at the heart of children's work in science, needs an element of trust on the part of the teacher that whatever the result something will be learned and like ICT, pupils will need to be left on their own for a while to make their own mistakes. The science coordinator also might have been part of the dramatic changes in primary science during the 1980s and 90s when it changed from one on the periphery to a core subject. They may have experience as a change agent and so be most useful as a partner.

The frequent concern of science coordinators is to encourage sufficient attention to be paid to AT1 — experimental and investigative science. For example, pupils should be given the opportunity to ask questions related to their work and use focused exploration and investigation to acquire scientific knowledge, understanding and skills; and use both first hand experience and secondary sources to obtain information. In order to do this they are recommended to use ICT to collect, store, retrieve and present scientific information. (See Figure 5.3)

You may wish to work out with the coordinator some ways in which she might encourage staff to use ICT towards these ends.

Areas of scientific learning including elements from the SCIENCE Programme of Study	Uses of ICT based on your school's equipment, software and peripherals — work this out with the coordinator — some suggestions in *italics*
Use their knowledge and understanding of science to explain and interpret a range of familiar phenomena.	Use word processors and drawing programs to describe findings. ICT can also support the scientific method of prediction, testing, drawing conclusions and displaying results. ICT can offer support at each stage, not just a bolt-on at the end.
Use standard measures and SI units appropriate to their work.	Set up survey sheets for recording in mm, Kg, ml, with parameters set to reject non SI units
Study life processes and relate their understanding of science to their personal health.	Use diary programmes to record own health and fitness. Analyse through charts and graphs. Virtual Frog dissection (two web sites) http://curry.edschool.Virginia.EDU/go/frog/ http://george.lbl.gov/ITG.hm.pg.docs/dissect/info.html
Consider the ways in which living things and the environment need protection.	Use CD ROMs for research, simulations for population growth studies The largest on-line environmental information service http://envirolink.org
Recognise reversible changes such as dissolving, melting, boiling, condensing, freezing and evaporating *cf* burning wood, wax, natural gas which are irreversible.	Use CD ROMs for research and use word processors and drawing programs to describe results.
Use a wide range of methods, including diagrams, drawings, graphs, tables and charts, to record and present information in a systematic manner.	Use of pre-made and purpose built databases Use spreadsheets for analysis Working with text, tables and graphs when both predicting and presenting results. IT offers a way of accessing useful support materials for teachers and pupils. Using CD ROM to find out information, communicating with others through the Internet / E-mail. Fossils web site http://recomputer.elecricfrog.co.uk/woods_fossils/Homepage.htm Natural History Museum web site http://www.nhm.ac.uk/ Volcano World web site http://volcano.und.nodak.edu
Know that some materials are better insulators than others; better electrical conductors than others. Group rocks according to their appearance, texture and permeability.	
The earth and beyond: its spin, day and night, shadows. Light travels from a source casts shadows; how it is received through the eye. Sound vibration which is not always visible, travels through a variety of materials	Use simulations for modelling when the experiments may be quick, slow, hazardous or out of reach. Models can be repeated frequently to aid understanding. Modelling software ranges from Diet, Human body, Space and the solar system NetSpace Project web site http://netspace.students.brown.edu/and NASA at http:/www.nasa.gov/ Earth & environmental science web site http://info.er.usgs.gov/network/science/earth/index.html (*See examples of light and space*)
Obtain evidence to test scientific ideas in a variety of ways	Use data-logging equipment to capture results in the testing stage. Use spreadsheet to record the exercise results
Sort various everyday materials, wood, rock, iron, aluminium, paper, polythene on the basis of their properties including hardness, strength, flexibility and magnetic behaviour and relate these to the everyday uses of these materials.	Use databases to categorise properties and sort into groups. Encouragement of close observation, development of classification skills and careful choice of language in constructing a database.

FIG 5.3
ICT and the science curriculum

Art, craft and design

The art coordinator may prove to be quite receptive to the increased use of the computer in order to further children's development in this subject and may well be persuaded that the use of the computer can:

- permit different ideas to be tried out quickly before deciding on a particular design and different stages in its development which can be saved and returned to when needed;
- allow cut and paste facilities to be used to isolate a particular area of the picture and sections of designs relocated, rotated and used to fill other areas;
- by scaling up and down adjust the size to allow it to be used for different purposes, for example reduction of an image to use in a repeating pattern;
- allow complex shapes to be rotated and viewed on the screen and this can help children gain an awareness of depth, shape and space;
- allow many different colour combinations to be tried in a short span of time and the luminosity of the computer screen gives the image a dramatic strength of colour, especially when used against a dark background;
- allow selected images to be printed and then form the basis of discussion for further development;
- provide an opportunity to use previously acquired skills to recreate textural effects of painting;
- allow several pictures to be viewed simultaneously and lead to discussions on what the original artists intended;
- with a video digitiser, be used to compile a picture library.

To assist teachers in their own schools, Birmingham City Education Department set out some example IT activities for different primary age groups. IT coordinators might wish to work with art coordinators to develop a more comprehensive list based on their own school's topic plan, software available and the art scheme of work (Figure 5.4).

It may be profitable to work with the art coordinator to give staff equipment, software and training to allow children access the advantages listed above. Further advice can be found in

Focus	Age/topic	IT activities	Applications
Communicating Developing the use of Save, fill and place functions, Mouse control and beginning to use different nib and brush tools to draw, colour and place regular shapes	Y1 Pattern Buildings and Places	Arrange regular shapes to form different outlines of buildings and skylines. Colour fill using day and night time colours. Freehand drawing of houses and factories.	Paintpot Deluxe
Develop use of different painting and drawing options and control in creating different qualities of line	Y2 Line and Tone, Islands	Initially experiment with creating straight, zigzagged, curved, wavy lines etc. Use these types of line to recreate a section of a landscape sketched by the children or one drawn by a famous artist	Paintpot Deluxe
Modelling/Designing	Y5 Pattern, The local area	Draw on screen a simple motif from sketches made of natural patterns. Copy this image and repeat a number of times. Place the motifs in various linear and rotating arrangements, forming a pattern. Combine shape with colour as a feature of the pattern. Show the chosen pattern imposed on an outline shape of a garment to be decorated with it	Paintspa Rembrandt Paintbrush
Communicating/Modelling	Y6 Texture, The root creature	Create a linear image of a root, save it and copy it. On the second image change and add lines to begin to transform the root into a creature. Copying the image again and repeat the process until the transformation from root to creature is complete. Use the series of images as designs for 3D work.	Paintspa Rembrandt Paintbrush

(Birmingham LEA, 1996)

FIG 5.4
Art, crafts and design and ICT planning

Areas of learning and experience including elements from the Programmes of Study for art, craft and design.	Uses of ICT based on your school's equipment, software and peripherals — work this out with the coordinator — some suggestions in *italics*
Pupils' understanding of art, craft and design should be developed through activities that bring together requirements from both investigating and making and knowledge and understanding	Use of CD ROM collections of art images and Clip Art drawings which can be manipulated to be part of further designs. Using ICT as a stimulus for developing art and design activities and accessing the work of artists for example through the web site at Le WebLouvre http://www.smartweb.fr/louvre/index.html
Introducing children to drawing, painting, print making, photography, sculpture, textiles, graphic design, architecture from the locality, the past and present, and a variety of cultures.	Using computer graphics as a stimulus for activities using other media. Using cameras, video digitisers, scanners and the photocopier. Details of over 46 art-related web server can be found at: http://sunsite.unc.edu/cisco/art.html
Pattern and texture	Art packages which allow cut and paste / airbrush.
Colour matching and how colour is mixed	Paint packages which encourage the experimentation with many different colour combinations.
Different approaches to art, individual, groups, whole class	By saving sections of computer art work both group and whole class works can be created simultaneously.
Express feelings and ideas record observations design and make images	Scaling images and dropping them into word processors

FIG 5.5
ICT and the art, craft and design curriculum

Music

IT in the Music National Curriculum Orders

Key Stage 1

1. Pupils should be given opportunities to:
   make appropriate use of IT to record sounds.

Key Stage 2

1. Pupils should be given opportunities to:
   make appropriate use of IT to explore and record sounds.

Attainment Target 1: Performing and composing
compose music for specific purpose and use notation(s) and, where appropriate, use information technology, to explore, develop and revise musical ideas.

The impact of electronic equipment, recorders, players and computers on music in schools is significant. Today you no longer have to be a performer to be a composer; further, it is not always necessary for you to get players together in order to hear the results of composed work (Walker, 1995). As IT coordinator you might do well to work with the coordinator for music to devise activities which bring together both performing and composing along with listening and appraising music. You may need to consider the purchase of specialist equipment such as extension speakers for the computers, cassette and CD players, video tape recorders and electronic keyboards with MIDI connections. A four track reorder, once out of reach for most primary schools now comes as standard with many synthesizers.

One of the big advantages that information technology has brought about is the kudos that it has given music in schools (Dempsey, 1995). Gone are the days when a certain amount of fun was made, especially of boys who were involved in music. Technology has bridged the gap and given status and motivation to music makers. Pupils see electronic keyboards at the centre of the pop music industry and computers feature in pop videos and in the setting up of concerts from the playing order to the creation of lighting effects. The music coordinator may be persuaded that if pupils can be encouraged to compose music on a computer in an idiom of their choice, then they may move on to all sorts of music making.

Examples of the way in which ICT can be used to help children achieve in music include:

- recording and exploring everyday sounds;
- using a drum machine to show different rhythms;
- telling a story through a sequence of sounds;
- recording and hearing their own part in a performance;
- change and distort the pitch, duration, dynamics, tempo, timbre, texture, of sounds by means of an electronic keyboard or by means of software;
- use recorded (sampled) sounds as a resource for composition;
- through tapes and CDs explore music from different places and times from European classical, folk and popular music, the regions of GB and cultures across the world;
- compare instruments;
- using simple composing software such as Compose (SEMERC); Notate (Longman);
- Using sounds in a multimedia presentation Ultima (SEMERC)/ Magpie (Longman) Illuminus (RM).

Web sites include:

Music web servers	http://www.cco.caltech.edu/~musicpgm
Planet starchild	http://www.streams.com/starchild/
Music resources	http://www.yahoo.co.uk/entertainment/music/Independent_music_resources
New Zealand Symphony Orchestra	http://www.nzso.co.nz/
The Rolling Stones	http://www.stones.com/ (download 'Sympathy for the Devil')

Using IT to record and explore: (taken from *Primary Music — a pupil's entitlement to* IT (NCET, 1996)	
Will help pupils to: To use and investigate sounds and structures	*By, for example:* using a tape recorder to capture sounds from a variety of sources for discussion and analysis; using amplifier tone controls or settings when sampling software, to discover how sounds can be adjusted; using an amplifier with reverberation or special effects; hardware or software to investigate how sounds can be modified; using an electronic keyboard to try out and select from a range of sounds or mix different sounds together; adjusting the settings on an electronic keyboard to make new sounds; comparing different combinations of keyboard auto-accompany= accompaniment features or computer; sequencer tracks to investigate textures; using software or an electronic keyboard with a record function to re-order sections of music.
Refine and enhance performance and composition	*By, for example:* recording their own or other pupils' work now in progress in order to discuss and refine material; recording finished work for presentation or use with poems, dance, art work and drama; using a tape recorder, electronic keyboard or computer to supply one part of a live performance; using a computer program to draw a score of their composition; using microphones and amplifiers to enhance a performance; using computer software programs to develop specific keyboard and oral skills.
Extend their knowledge of different styles of music	*By, for example:* using a CD ROM to learn about the music and background of a variety of performers and composers; listening to and exploring examples of music on cassette tape, CD, CDs, video, radio; using electronic keyboard to investigate different auto accompaniment rhythm styles; using fax, e-mail or Internet browser to exchange musical ideas, materials and information with experts or other pupils.

Software sources can be found in the final chapter of this book.

You might consider introducing the music coordinator to the DfEE Music IT support group. The aims of this project are:

- to raise awareness of how different facets of IT can enhance and enable musical learning;

- to identify and disseminate good practice in the use of IT in the music classroom;
- to hold musical learning above technical expertise and to encourage simple but effective ways of using IT where appropriate;
- to provide practical ideas for teachers; and,
- to promote further research into the potential of music technology applications in music education.

As a result the project has produced 'The Music IT pack' available from NCET.

Geography

IT in the Geography National Curriculum Orders

Key Stage 1

Geographical Skills
Pupils should be taught to:
use secondary sources e.g. pictures, photographs (*including aerial photographs*), *books, videos, CD ROM encyclopaedia, to obtain information.*

Key Stage 2

Geographical Skills
Pupils should be taught to:
use IT to gain access to additional information sources to assist handling, classifying and presenting evidence, e.g. *recording fieldwork evidence on spreadsheets, using newspapers on CD ROM, using word processing and mapping packages.*

The coordinator for geography will be interested in the ways computers and other ICT equipment can help children to investigate the physical and human features of their surroundings; undertake studies that focus on geographical questions such as where is it? what is it like? how did it get like this? — record their direct experience, practical activities and fieldwork in the locality of the school; and assist in the development of skills and help them to know about places and themes (Figure 5.6).

Areas of learning and experience including elements from the Programme of Study for geography	Uses of ICT based on your school's equipment, software and peripherals — work this out with the coordinator — some suggestions in *italics*
To provide an opportunity to observe, collect, question, record and analyse information. To communicate ideas and information — observe, question, record and communicate ideas and information	Using CD ROM and prepared databases to find information. Working with text, tables, and pictures to create newspapers, reports and to represent information graphically. Planet Earth Home Page http://normandy.sandhills.cc.nc.us/numbers.html Hunger http://www.hunger.brown.edu/hungerweb
To understand terms such as hill, river, road, waterfalls, volcano, car parks woodland, traffic housing types, mapping the school playground, seas, cities valley, reservoirs, transport, industry	Use small hand-held computers to record field trips. Use computer pictures, photographs, videos, CD ROM encyclopaedia to obtain information. Adventure games Volcano World web site http://volcano.und.nodak.edu
Making a map route from home to school and beyond, supply of goods, patterns of development, links between towns, use of land	Introducing distance and route plotting programs. Using LOGO activities and geographical simulations to inform and stimulate enquiry and imagination.
Weather: sheltered and exposed sites, seasonal variations, temperature	Fieldwork (using portable computers) rain gauges/surveys with sensing equipment. Use of spreadsheets for analysis, ready made databases for information. Making a weather station.
Environmental issues, extremes of weather, seasonal weather patterns, variation in rainfall, proposals for a new supermarket, water pollution, building motorways	Video, Internet, newspapers stored on CD ROM, TV and radio simulations (population growth). Working with text, tables, and pictures to create newspapers, letters and to represent information graphically. Earth and environmental science web site http://info.er.usgs.gov/network/science/earth/index.html Greenpeace http://www.greenpeace.org.uk
Studies of different countries Studies of two localities	Facts, history and beautiful images of Puerto Rico at the web site http://puertorico.unaid.com/facts.html Use of video, e-mail links, telephone, fax Use of doomsday material Schools on the web Low Bentham CP School http://cres1.lancs.ac.uk/~esarie/school.htm Langley Junior & Infants http:www-bprc.mps.ohio-state.edu/cgi/hpp/langleyji.html

FIG 5.6
ICT and the geography curriculum

Many CD ROMs have been published which set out to make children aware that the world extends beyond their own locality and that places exist within a broader geographical context. This could be a good starting point to work with the geography coordinator and from then to set about listing ways in which ICT can be useful to teachers in the geography curriculum.

History

IT in the History National Curriculum Orders

Key Stage 2

Study Unit 3b: Britain since 1930
Changes in technology and transport
Changes in industry and transport, including the impact of new technology, e.g. motor cars, computers, space travel.

The history coordinator will be pleased to work with you to find ways for children to use ICT to inform their knowledge and understanding so that they can develop an awareness of the past and a way of presenting and investigating aspects of history.

Various projects run by NCET have attempted to identify the pupils' entitlement to IT in history. The National Curriculum requires history students to be provided with opportunities to use IT. IT can help pupils to:

- ask historical questions;
- investigate change, cause and consequence;
- assess and use a wide range of sources;
- organise information and ideas and communicate effectively.

This is done by providing examples and advice on:

- identifying changes using databases;
- setting up enquiries using a CD ROM;
- analysing causes using a drawing package;
- structuring extended writing using a word processor. (See Figure 5.7)

Areas of learning and experience including elements from the Programme of Study for history	Uses of ICT based on your school's equipment, software and peripherals — work this out with the coordinator — some suggestions in *italics*
Develop an awareness of the past and the ways it is different from the present. Set their study in a chronological framework and understand some of the ways in which we find out about the past.	Using CD ROM and prepared databases to find information Using prepared databases, LOGO activities and historical simulations to stimulate enquiry and imagination
The past through clothes, jobs, transport, diet, household objects, houses, shops, entertainment.	Documents and printed sources, artefacts, pictures, photographs, music, buildings and sites Working with text and pictures to create newspapers, letters, stories and to design artefacts
Sense of chronology: Terms such as old, new, after, long ago, (use different fonts), days of the week, court, monarch, parliament, nation, civilisations, invasions, conquest, settlement, conversion, slavery, trade, industry, law, ancient, modern, BC, AD, century, decade.	Creation of time-line (printing on continuous paper) Concept keyboard overlays
Changes in their own lives and those of their family. The past beyond living memory.	Tape record interview with grandparents, older people.
Famous men and women, rulers, saints, artists, engineers, explorers, inventors, pioneers.	Documents and printed sources, artefacts, pictures, photographs, music, buildings and sites
Past events of different types — local and national events, events in other countries, commemorated events, religious festivals, Olympic games The reason and results of historical events, situations and changes	Local resources/video Communicate their awareness and understanding
Romans, Anglo-Saxons, Vikings, Tudor times, Ancient Greeks, Second World War	Computer-aided learning packages dealing with different periods CD ROM resources
Stories and eyewitness accounts — why people did things, why events happened and what happened as a result. Ideas, beliefs, attitudes of people in the past, the experiences of men and women; and the cultural, social, religious and ethnic diversity of the societies studied.	Pictures, written accounts, films, television programmes, plays, songs, reproduction of objects, museum displays Range of sources of information including CD ROM Use of portable (hand-held) computers on museum, field visits
History from a variety of perspectives — political; economic; technological and scientific; social; religious; cultural and aesthetic.	TV and video Texts and images http://aristotle2.isu.edu/clubhome/drking.html http:www.luc.edu/~scilib/jessci.html Welcome to the White House web site http://www.whitehouse.gov/ (see Royal Favourites) or to No 10 Downing St http://www.prime-minister.gov.uk/

FIG 5.7
ICT and the history curriculum

Joan's Royal Favourites and Links http://www.xs4all.nl/~kvenjb/favour.htm

Joan's Royal Favourites & Links Page

My main hobby is **royalty in history**: terrible tsars, sadistic sultans, deranged dukes, paranoid princes and crazy caesars. Some of them are described in my royalty in history page and my montly updated alliterative mad monarchs series, which have recently received some honourable mentions. I have recently added a FAQ (*frequently asked questions*). This page describes all my **favourites**: my favourite royalty in history links, my favourite books, my favourite royalty in history magazines and my favourite royal in history: Eleanor of Aquitaine!

This page can best be viewed with NETSCAPE 3.0.

My favourite *royal in history*:

Eleanor of Aquitaine (~1122-1204)

Duchess Eleanor of Aquitaine was an intelligent and emancipated woman living in the dark middle ages. Although it is a conventional rule that all ladies of high rank should be described as beautiful, all sources agree that Eleanor of Aquitaine really *was* beautiful. In addition, she was the richest heiress of France and became successively queen of France and England.

Eleanor was a granddaughter of William IX of Aquitaine (1070-1127), who was one of the first and most famous troubadours. He was a cheerful man and an ardent lover of women, who joined the First Crusade. Later he "abducted" the wife of the viscount of Châtellerault, Dangereuse, and although he could not marry her, Dangereuse managed to have *her* daughter Aenor married to *his* eldest son William X (1099-1137) in 1121. They had two daughters, Eleanor and Petronilla, and a son, William Aigret. Eleanor resembled both William IX and Dangereuse; she possessed the same intelligence, gaiety, restlessness and will power. The court of William IX was the centre of western European culture: the ducal family was entertained by jongleurs, storytellers and troubadours. Unlike most of her contemporaries, male and especially female, Eleanor was carefully educated and she was an excellent student. Eleanor's happy childhood ended with the subsequent deaths of her mother, her little brother and - in 1137 - her father.

(Reproduced with permission. Source: http://www.lib.byu.edu/~rdh/eurodocs/cite.html)

Design and technology

The coordinator for design and technology will be interested in ways in which you can involve ICT in helping children to develop designing and making skills and gain knowledge and understanding in order to help them design and make products. You may be able to work out ways together in which computers can help in the process (Figure 5.8).

Areas of learning and experience including elements from the Programme of Study for Design and Technology	Uses of ICT based on your school's equipment, software and peripherals — work this out with the coordinator — some suggestions in *italics*
Assignments in which they design and make products	Drawing programme to make drawings of their ideas CD ROM, to see what has been made before
Focused practical tasks in which they practice particular skills, activities in which they investigate, disassemble and evaluate simple products.	Graphing program to show their results
Clarify ideas through discussion Develop their ideas through shaping, assembling and rearranging materials and components Develop and communicate ideas, identify strengths and weaknesses	Using IT to research the task, CD ROM, to see what has been made before, and how the challenge was met Graphing program to show their results
Knowledge and understanding materials, control, structures, products and applications, quality, health and safety, vocabulary	Using ICT to research the task, CD ROM, to see what has been made before, and how the challenge was met
Select appropriate materials, tools and techniques — work with reclaimed material, textiles, food and construction kits	CD ROM to research into the task Vegetarian recipes web site http://www.vegsource.com/
Work independently and in teams	Work independently and in teams on the computer
Consider appearance, function, safety and reliability when developing proposals Generate ideas, considering the users and the purposes for which they are designing, evaluate design ideas and indicate improvements	The use of ICT to support the children's evaluation of their work, and the report writing Select files and images, web site (see 'Friends of the Earth') http://www.oltc.edu.au/case2.htm Working with ICT when a table of results is appropriate

FIG 5.8
ICT and the design and technology curriculum

Friends of the Earth Home Page http://www.foe.co.uk/

England, Wales and Northern Ireland

Latest Press Release...... 18 Feb 1998

MILLENNIUM ECO-VILLAGE: FINE UNTIL YOU LOOK NEXT DOOR

Climate Change

Climate for change, or just hot air? FOE's view on the Kyoto deal and more...

Wild Places! On The Web

Help protect wildlife sites where YOU live ..

The Chemical Release Inventory

Find the Pollution in Your Backyard ..

Cars Cost The Earth!

Test drive our Virtual Java Car

Wild Woods!

Stop The Destruction Of The Snowforests

Tomorrow's World

Friends of the Earth's blueprint for a sustainable future.

We rely almost entirely on concerned individuals to fund our vital work.
Please join in & help us today - the Earth needs all the Friends it can get!

(Reproduced with permission.)

Cross-curricular uses of ICT

In order to achieve certain expected outcomes from lessons and other activities targeted software has been detailed above. There are many programs however which enhance more than one aspect of the curriculum simultaneously and can lead to work at and away from the keyboard for sustained periods. Mathematical investigations, creative writing, historical research, scientific experiments, drama, music and PE can all be stimulated by simulation and adventure programs (Straker and Govier, 1996). Further details can be found in the resources section.

Chapter 6

What IT coordinators need to know about teachers and computers

*Using IT makes teachers take a fresh look at how they teach and the ways in which students learn.*

Somekh (1989), Watson et al. (1993), Ragsdale (1991)

Teachers' competence in using ICT

How much do all teachers have to know about using and communicating with computers, and what should their levels of personal skills be in order to teach effectively? The necessary level of teachers' subject knowledge is a matter of some debate in all curriculum areas. Recent attention to the degree subjects for applicants for PGCE courses, the new TTA standards, which define a proxy level 8 in the pupils' National Curriculum in IT as a requirement for qualified teachers status and *OFSTED's* references to teachers' own skills, all imply that student achievement is allied to teachers' own level of knowledge and skills. NCET have developed seven statements of competence in information technology for teachers. These are under three main headings: framework, implementation and broadening. These may be of use to you, as coordinator, so you can better estimate the progress your teachers may make in this area against a wider background. The process during which teachers develop these attributes is not expected to be sequential but cyclical. I have adapted these statements to meet current needs and to suit the primary teachers I know.

Framework of understanding

A competent primary teacher could be said to have:

- **an understanding** of the ways in which information and communications technology contribute to teaching and learning in Key Stages 1 and 2, acquired through:
  - **knowledge** that ICT contribute to the teacher's own personal learning and professional development;
  - **belief** that ICT should contribute to the learning of children;
  - the **ability** to review and reflect critically on the implementation of the above and thus add to her/his understanding.
- an **understanding** of the developing nature of ICT capability and an awareness that it is integral to the whole structure and purposes of the National Curriculum, acquired through:
  - **awareness** of appropriate ICT resources (both in breadth and depth) and a knowledge of when and when not to use them;
  - **knowledge** of the ways in which ICT subject and cross-curricular applications assist in the attainment of National Curriculum objectives;
  - **appreciation** that the ICT culture continues to evolve and grow rapidly;
  - the **ability** to review and reflect critically on the above and thus increase personal understanding.

What does this say about what teachers ought to know and be able to do and how can you help teachers to achieve this? Teachers should be aware of the many ways in which teaching and learning with information and communications technology contributes to children's understanding in a number of curricular areas. This could be encouraged by teaming up with the coordinators of other subject areas as suggested in the previous chapter, through inviting in outside speakers, by showing video clips or organising trips to other schools. Discussions with parents can be useful for many will support the conclusion that it is essential that ICT should contribute to the learning of children and fit them for the world of work.

Through staffroom discussion teachers will variously develop the ability to review and reflect critically on the implementation of their aims in this area but may need some encouragement to focus on the improvements in their teaching that they may need to make to be most effective.

What personal use do teachers in your team make of information and communications technology? Do they strive to create worksheets illustrated with clip-art picture prompts, label displays, make banner headlines over children's displays, create class lists for recording the collection of money, recording marks, do they use a database of contact addresses for the class or regularly write up their lesson plans by using a computer? Do teachers search the Internet for teaching materials? Does the school organise its reports or records of achievement by using IT, what about records of team games or keeping the score on sports day? Are standard letters to parents word processed so that they can easily be amended and used again, is the school on-line to the LEA for easy transfer of financial information? Do teachers know this?

Tasks for teachers to improve their personal capability	
Types of question which might prompt ICT solutions	Task
What a you hoping to achieve? Can you write down the problem in a different way?	Focus on outcomes, communicating needs
What information do you already know?	Logical ways of summarising information
Is there enough information and could you get any more? Is there too much information? Which might be the most important? Have you used all the information?	Data handling, logical sequencing, problem solving techniques. Seeking sources of information
Have you broken the problem down into smaller parts? Do you notice any patterns?	Using branching programs
Would it help to put things in a different order?	Sorting
Had you thought of changing any variables — one at a time? What about trying a particular case? What about making a guess and seeing what happens?	'What if' modelling
Are there others with whom you could discuss the problem?	Using communications technology
Are there any general trends?	Databases/spreadsheets
Would a graph help?	Data handling programs

Implementation in the classroom

In the classroom a competent primary teacher can:

- **use** the computer and communications technology to support everyday classroom activities at an appropriate level and assess the learning which takes place;
- **ensure** progression of pupils' learning through sensitive intervention;
- **bring** to this an evaluative framework that enables critical reflection on how ICT changes the teaching and learning processes.

In implementing ICT in school a primary teacher can and does demonstrate:

- **an ability to stimulate children's thirst for knowledge through using communications technology**;
- an **understanding** of why ICT is being used and convey this to her/his pupils;
- an **ability** to plan learning activities in which ICT is an integral and contributory element;
- an **awareness** of the limitations and value of the use of ICT and the ability to convey this to the pupils through their learning activities;
- the **ability** to develop pupils' ICT capability;
- the **ability** to review critically pupils' experiences with ICT.

Can you, as coordinator, intervene in the planning process to ensure that ICT are recognised as an integral and contributory element in each of the classes for which you bear responsibility? Can your teachers be encouraged to use the computer to support everyday classroom activities at an appropriate level and assess the learning which takes place, and ensure progression? Over a period this might become second nature to those you advise along with discussion around the limitations and value of the use of ICT.

Much teacher time has been invested in the past few years in helping teachers develop their skills in assessing pupils' capability across whole the curriculum. Can you unlock this learning and help teachers to apply it to ICT along with the ability to review critically pupils' experiences with ICT?

Coordinators' check questions for individual teachers	
	Y/N comments
Do teachers plan and prepare adequately for use of the computer within lessons? How well do teachers plan the integration of the use of the computer with other classroom activities? Do they encourage their children to communicate with other children in different parts of the world? Can they tell you the next piece of software that they will introduce? Have they planned for this?	
Do teachers spend enough time working with and observing children whilst they are using the computer? Do they spend sufficient time listening to and talking with the children about their past work with the computer?	
How many teachers can resist intervening when children are trying to solve a problem for themselves?	
In lessons do teachers generally allow time for children to consider various options? Do their pupils use ICT to solve problems?	
Are groups organised so that particular children do not dominate within a group?	
Do teachers assess and keep a record of the children's progress with their computer work?	
Are the programs selected flexible enough to match the needs of each individual child?	

Developing ICT competence

Continued development through school-based and external INSET should mean that proficient teachers will be able to:

- adapt to curricular changes, to learners' needs and to emerging technology;
- maintain a holistic understanding of ICT in the curriculum;
- continue to implement and evaluate ICT-supported learning activities.

The proficient primary teacher can and does:

- develop her/his professional curiosity concerning how young children learn and the contribution that ICT has to offer in order to improve standards of achievement;
- use ICT in context and for an effective purpose naturally, as a personal tool in her/his teaching, and for associated professional activities such as record-keeping, lesson development, assessment and school administration;
- make effective decisions on the use of ICT in the context of:

  intervention strategies;
  problem solving;
  resource management;
  task management;
  information skills;
  social implications;
  health and safety education;
  special educational needs;
  equal opportunities;
  differentiation.
- seek opportunities for updating personal ICT skills and receive professional support;
- participate in curriculum development in school;
- collaborate with colleagues in ICT-related professional development.

This set of competences clearly represents a staff who have been 'future proofed'. For teachers to be able to adapt to the many curricular changes they will need to maintain their holistic understanding of ICT in the curriculum, and continue to implement and evaluate ICT-supported learning activities.

Technical capability in ICT

The technical capability of teachers is varied but will progress throughout their involvement with using ICT with children. Coordinators working with headteachers may be able to build into teachers' programmes of work opportunities to gain general skills, understanding of specific software applications and learning to use the word processor efficiently.

One of the best ways to help teachers develop these personal skills is to encourage them to use the computer as a means to solve problems and to answer their own questions. It is not an easy step for managers to stand back from their traditional role as answer providers. Yet if teachers are to become autonomous learners and good problem solvers within ICT they need to take increasing responsibility for discovering their own solutions to problems.

It may well be that researching a CD ROM, 'surfing' the Internet, using a spreadsheet for an accounts task or a wordprocessor for a report is appropriate. Can you let your colleagues discover this for themselves (or think they did?).

However, teachers may also be keen to develop technical proficiency and an audit may lead you to decide just what skills may need to be taught.

Name of Teacher ______________________							Audit of skills
How would you estimate your ability to	I=expert 4=competent 7=no experience/ability						
load a Word Processing program type in text and print it out	I	2	3	4	5	6	7
save, load and edit files	I	2	3	4	5	6	7
justify text/set headers/paginate	I	2	3	4	5	6	7
change fonts/underline/embolden/italicise/colour text/convert case	I	2	3	4	5	6	7
move text about, use a spell checker/thesaurus	I	2	3	4	5	6	7
set up and modify tables, text boxes, import borders, graphics and files	I	2	3	4	5	6	7
use find/search and replace features	I	2	3	4	5	6	7
connect to the Internet	I	2	3	4	5	6	7
search for documents on the World Wide Web	I	2	3	4	5	6	7
send and receive e-mail messages and files	I	2	3	4	5	6	7
create or modify a webpage	I	2	3	4	5	6	7
use a ready-made spreadsheet	I	2	3	4	5	6	7
set up a spreadsheet for own purposes	I	2	3	4	5	6	7
use a ready-made database	I	2	3	4	5	6	7
set up a database to solve a problem	I	2	3	4	5	6	7
use LOGO programming language	I	2	3	4	5	6	7
use a roamer/pip/pixie	I	2	3	4	5	6	7
set up and use remote sensors	I	2	3	4	5	6	7

As you will see from Chapter 8, some of these skills are growing in importance. The consultation for the National Grid for Learning (DfEE, 1997) has as a target that by 2002 around 75 per cent of teachers and 50 per cent of pupils will have their own e-mail addresses. By this date general administrative communications to schools by the UK Education Departments, Ofsted and non-departmental public bodies, and the collection of data from schools, should cease to be paper-based. From these surveys of your colleagues' skills and areas of competence you can then draw up a practical plan for in-service training (see Figure 6.1).

Some progress will need to be made toward the competences in this chapter if teachers are to cope with these conditions.

Staff training needs identified from survey				
Software/hardware	Skill/area identified	Staff/names	Training date on/off premises/individual group	Resources required/costs estimate/success criteria

FIG 6.1
Planning INSET

Chapter 7

What IT coordinators need to know about choosing computers, software and peripherals

Much of the technical advice below is taken directly from a series of leaflets published as *Choosing and Using IT Equipment* by NCET. With permission of NCET the leaflets used include: *Computer Security*; *Evaluating CD-ROM titles*; *Local Area Networks*; *Using the Internet*; *Making Multimedia*; *Modems*; *Portable Computers*; *Printers*; *Cd-ROM drives*; *Data Logging*; *and Desktop, Computers*. Other sources are acknowledged within the text.

In order that coordinators can be aware of the latest information which will inform their purchases and help them to make the best use of ICT equipment, NCET are offering a discounted copy of the latest of the above publications to readers using the cut-out voucher found at the end of the book.

In Chapter 2 the IT coordinator was clearly identified as the member of staff who need to be prepared to offer 'first aid' technical help to teachers. Some understanding of the various functions of the machines and their connectivity is implied and hence this chapter is meant to be of assistance in sorting out the basics. Moreover your advice will (or should) be sought when new purchases are planned and in the best run schools you should be able to develop a short-, medium-, and long-term view when budgeting the resources devoted to this area. Hence information on computer hardware is presented here as an overview — it will be too little for some readers and too complex for others. Those of you faced with the prospect of advising the headteacher and governors on highly technical matters are recommended to read the latest information supplied by manufacturers. Coordinators who are new to the post might re-read this chapter in a year or so when they have become used to the problems involved.

Desktop computers

When do you replace worn out computers, with what and how much should you spend? Progress marches on. All computers eventually become out of date and more attractive machines with better features are always going to be available. This usually seems to happen within a few months of having made a major purchase (see comments by Real Time Club opposite). One option is to upgrade old computers by adding new chips. However, when you do this, only part of the computing process is improved, old software frequently needs a 'patch' for it to work in the new environment and unexpected effects on other programs can be the result. What is needed in most primary schools is a purchasing strategy to complement the clear uses for computers and peripherals you have specified in your ICT policy (Chapter 9).

As long as your school's development plan is clear and progressive you will be able to adopt a practical strategy, but without this it is pure guesswork.

> *Like any teaching resource, a computer is only as good as the teacher in charge of it. You're wasting your time buying a load of computers unless you know exactly what you want to do with them. You might as well buy several thousand pounds' worth of colouring books.* Palmer (1997)

But guess we must. In industry machines are given a four year lifespan. Many of our school computers need to work for 5–13 years. But how can coordinators decide if they are obsolete?

- What is the record of breakdowns and malfunctions?
  – this implies that you have a record for each machine!
- What is the effect of any breakdown?
  – if the teacher hardly notices that the computer is missing, or if your repair system is so efficient it is only out of action for a day or so then this is minor

According to the Real Time Club, a computing think tank, schools spend just 0.86 per cent of their budgets on IT, compared with financial services businesses which invest an average 15 per cent of their budgets.

(Edwards, 1997)

  - if it causes wholesale disruption to a project then this is obviously far more serious
- What is the machine currently used for?
  - what is it not able to do, how fast is it, is it attractive to pupils?
- Is it going to be more and more difficult to effect repairs as time goes by and have software houses stopped producing programs for it?
  - for example this currently applies to Acorn models prior to the Archimedes

NCET recommend:

If any of your school's computers are obsolete then don't let them influence your future purchasing decisions. Bear in mind:

- The software already in use in your school

  Ignore obsolete machines — but how does the new purchase relate to software with which children and teachers are familiar? Will this new computer eventually be networked? Does your already existing software need to be able to work on this computer?
- The potential uses of the new computer

  Is it to connect to the Internet, play CD ROMs, stand alone in the library, be used largely as a word processor, offer different forms of experience, used across the whole school, reinforce already learned concepts, open up new curriculum areas (French in the primary school), for example?
- The software currently available and what is likely to be produced in the future

  What range of educational software is currently advertised for this computer — are new titles promised?
- The ease of use of the machine

  Is it mouse-driven and already loaded with easily accessible software? Would pupils and staff need to learn a new set of skills or could they adapt what they know already?
- The ease of connection to existing printers and other peripherals

  Check that you will not have to buy new printers when you purchase your new computer.

- The price

  Global market share is reflected in the price — IBM compatibles having a range of manufacturers are the cheapest to buy and Acorn the most expensive. The costs of technical support and training need also to be taken into account. Without the ability to use CD ROMs your new equipment will be of limited value.

Choosing a PC

> What governors need to do is first help the teaching team to put together a forward looking IT plan, and then decide whether, and how it can be achieved through proper management of the budget. They might, for example, decide that in five years' time the whole school will be networked with a machine in every teaching area, and fibre-optic cabling between separated buildings. Although doing all of that right now might be too expensive, knowing the eventual destination means that every IT decision should be a step towards it. (Other ostensibly non-IT decisions will be affected too. If a room is to be replastered, for example, then it may be sensible to put in extra power points and cable paths against the time when they will be needed which only underlines the fact that governing body groups such as the premises sub-committee cannot work in isolation from each other). Haigh (1994)

PC checklist

If you are thinking of buying in the near future, look carefully at the specifications of machines on offer (Figure 7.1). Various NCET publications exist to assist you in your decision and you should read them and consider some of the issues they raise as below:

Is the PC value for money?
Does it come with appropriate software?
Are the sellers reliable?
Do they understand education?
Is there good, accessible telephone support?
What does it consist of?
What happens if the dealer goes out of business next month?
Is there a leasing scheme and is it value for money?
Is it possible to get the machine upgraded, repaired or components replaced?

Hardware purchasing plan: software needed Software licences: individual stand-alone copies needed Part of budget plan for 19_. Governors' long term planning for _					
Hardware/software required: manufacturer, software publisher	Function/purpose learning outcomes	Where will it be used — licence required?	Price (ex VAT)	Purchase date proposed financial year	To be financed by

FIG 7.1
Hardware purchasing plan

If you economise on support, does it exist within the school?
Will the machine be supported by your local education authority or local information technology centre?
How well does the machine harmonise with existing technology in the school?

Further advice is offered by Coupland (1995) to help IT coordinators to decide amongst various types of computer, such as IBM PCs, Acorns and the Apple Mac series.

Other ICT equipment

Your advice may also be sought on the purchase and use of a variety of peripherals. Advice is readily available from LEA IT centres and NCET publications. Below I have summarised several pamphlets from a number of sources — but principally NCET's *Choosing and Using IT Equipment* which is regularly updated to help IT coordinators and others responsible for purchasing equipment to make appropriate choices for their circumstances.

Portable computers

- UK sales of portables are booming as they become general purpose machines. These machines bring diversity and mobility. With portables the technology goes where it is needed — in classrooms, laboratories, sports areas and on field trips.
- Giving teachers easy access to computers in their own teaching areas encourages and improves the use of ICT in the wider curriculum. They also bring flexibility. Not everyone needs a powerful computer all the time.
- **Notebook** computers that usually have both an internal hard disk and a floppy disk drive should run all the standard software. They are available in all three types of computer currently found in schools: IBM PC compatibles, Apple Macintosh and Acorn Archimedes and run on internal rechargeable batteries. They are mostly A4 telephone directory size and weigh 2–3kg. Colour is available but costs more.

McTaggart (1997) reports that reading standards at a number of inner-city schools have risen dramatically over the past two years with portable computers central to the improvement. Six hundred 8 and 9-year-olds took part in an project designed to improve their literacy and numeracy skills for more than a year using Acorn Pocket Book hand held computers designed to encourage parental involvement and motivate the pupils to learn. The children, who came from 14 east London schools, developed stories and poems and finished the tasks at home. In the following days the completed work was then down loaded to desktop computers and printed at school.

- **Palmtops** are pocket-size computers, smaller, lighter and have a much longer battery life. The keyboards have the standard QWERTY layout but are tiny: screens are black and white and about a quarter of the area of a notebook computer. Batteries are usually the standard AA size and can last for 10–50 hours depending on the model of machine and pattern of use. A back-up battery system is an essential. Basic office software, plus a diary or address book, is embedded in most of these machines.
- **Low cost word processors** are a compromise between notebooks and palmtops. Compromises have been made to keep them cheap. The screen and full-size keyboard are on the upper surface and there is no lid. They do not have a built-in hard disk or floppy disk drive and they use AA batteries. They come with a word processor and organiser software.

Several NCET projects show that portables can catalyse major changes in teaching and learning styles as they become personal tools to pick up and use. The machines are frequently used flexibly and much of the work seen is collaborative. Reports show a variety of uses from the production of a collaborative *Book of the World* in a multi-cultural school detailing children's own background and customs to nursery pupils, focusing on the adventures of two teddy bears who visit the children's homes. Some older pupils are reported to have learned keyboard skills, helping each other with redrafting; using computer print-out and keyboards which helped them to realise the importance of grammar, punctuation and presentation. Less able pupils were motivated by achieving parity with their peers in terms of their results. Schools often sought the active involvement of parents as part of a policy to encourage support for the children's education at home (NCET, 1995).

Printers

As we all know, no matter how successful the activity around the computer monitor, children are always keen to see their work on the wall, to take it home to show parents, or put it in their project folders as a permanent record of their achievement. Moreover, most children when composing written work need a 'hard copy' of their drafts to discuss with other people in order to attain a high standard. Thus a printer is a necessity for primary classrooms. Printers will need to work with a range of software packages to print plain text, desktop published documents, pictures and graphics. Important decisions about how printers are to be used must be made before you define the selection criteria.

Selecting a suitable printer can be a difficult process. There is a bewildering selection of types, models and manufacturers, and a wide range not only in purchase and running costs but also in print quality, speed and reliability.

NCET advice includes:

- When choosing a printer to match classroom needs, you will need to consider a number of factors:
- Connectivity – stand-alone shared or networked facilities
- Performance – print quality and speed
- Design quality – robust and easy to operate
- Compatibility – the ability to work with all your computers and software
- Flexibility – the ability to be moved to and work in different settings
- Colour – capability and quality
- Optional extras
- Costs – capital and recurrent

As colour printers fall in price there is increasing interest in making them the standard classroom printer. There are occasions however, when a black and white printer is a better choice (such as when the high quality of a laser printer is needed) where low running costs are vital, or where speed is a major consideration. Almost all colour printing is the result of mixing the four basic colours of yellow, cyan, magenta and black. We assume that the colour we will see in print will be the same as on the screen, but this is never the case.

The main types of printers

- **9-pin dot-matrix printers** impress ink from a ribbon on to the paper. More modern 24-pin printers are faster and produce better print quality. There are colour versions too, which use a 4-colour ribbon, often costing only a few pounds more than the black ink model. The advantage of these printers is that they are cheap to buy and run, and work with a wide variety of software. Print quality soon drops as the ribbon wears out. Print speed is relatively slow, especially the colour versions, and some models are rather noisy.

- **Inkjet printers** spray through a matrix of fine nozzles onto the paper. Running costs are higher because of the liquid ink cartridges. They are quiet and very convenient to use. Colour models are also available. This type of printer will also print OHP transparencies (on special films).
- **Laser printers** have a higher resolution creating very sharp images. However toner cartridges are expensive and running costs per sheet are similar to those of a Xerox-type photocopier.

CD ROM drives

Coordinators will know that a great deal of primary software is now advertised as coming on CD ROM. To access these titles your school will need a CD ROM drive. NCET produce a guideline for those considering buying these units that are shown in precis below.

- A CD ROM can store a great quantity of data, around 600Mb, which is equivalent to 250,000 A4 pages of text. They can store photographs, sound, motion video and playback software to present these materials to the user. Multimedia PCs have an internal CD ROM drive housed within the system unit case, a sound card and speakers. Other computers can be upgraded by adding a CD ROM drive in a free disk bay or by connecting one externally as a separate box.
- Choosing a CD ROM drive will be determined by the following things: the price you can afford to pay, the kinds of discs you wish to play on your drive, which interface card you will be using with the drive, any extra features you require and the amount of 'future proofing' you wish to have.
- Photo CD has been developed by Kodak to store up to 100 photographs on a CD. High street retailers such as Boots

can send pictures to a bureau that will transfer them to a Photo CD.

- Conventional CD ROM discs store different sorts of data, such as sound and pictures, in different places on the disc and these are read at different times. CD ROM XA (eXtended Architecture) interleaves audio and visual material in the same track on the disc.
- CDI (Compact Disc Interactive) is a format developed by Philips, and like CD ROM it is able to store and manipulate text, sound, illustrations and moving video. CDI discs must be played on a dedicated CDI player with a conventional television monitor.
- There are three disc loading mechanisms. Top-load drives, tray-loading drives and others use a 'caddy' to transport the disc. Tray-loading drives, are becoming the industry standard.

A number of specialist computer journals regularly carry out tests and publish the results on current and new CD ROM drives. *PC Magazine* and *Personal Computer World* deal exclusively with IBM PC compatible products, *Macworld* and *MacUser* with the Apple Macintosh and *Acorn User* with Acorn machines. Journals such as *Educational Computing and Technology* give less technical advice but with an educational slant. There are also a number of new CD ROM specific titles such as *CD ROM World* that carry cross-platform reviews.

Multimedia

Multimedia combines words, pictures, photographs, audio and video in digital form. Schools are beginning to encounter multimedia in the form of commercially published CD ROMs which can be used in the library or classroom. However, using published materials is only half the story for children can also create their own multimedia software. Just as they currently create their own newspapers, it is also possible for them to build multimedia programs that have many of the features of commercial CD ROMs.

Multimedia development provides an opportunity for students to communicate ideas and present information in a variety of forms. NCET (1996) claim that developing multimedia can help students to:

- develop a visual literacy;
- work collaboratively;
- consider the structure and organisation of material;
- develop a deeper appreciation of published materials;
- handle non-sequential information such as hypertext.

It relates strongly to the *Communicating and Handling of Information* strand of the National Curriculum for IT.

Computer security

Your school's computers will be used for a wide variety of purposes, from curriculum development and delivery to library records, pupil records, timetabling, administration and finance. Convenience and flexibility, however, do create an underlying complexity and the need for thoroughness and vigilance in managing networks reliably and securely. As in business, schools need to consider what would happen if confidential data was obtained by unauthorised persons.

Data Protection Act (1984)

This Act sets out standards for the holding and processing of personal data (data referring to identifiable individuals) on a computer. These standards are set out in eight principles which, in practical terms, mean that schools must:

- explain to persons giving information what it will be used for;
- register all use of personal data (such as for staff and pupil records);
- only use the data in accordance with the register entries and for the purposes understood by the person concerned;
- limit the scope to relevant and adequate data about individuals;
- ensure that the data is accurate and up to date;
- destroy the data when it is no longer needed;
- allow individuals (or a parent/guardian) to see their records on request and to challenge any inaccuracies;
- keep the data secure.

(NCET, 1996)

There is no such thing as 100 per cent security, whether for computer-based or manual systems: all that can be done is to reduce the probability of misuse or loss.

The main threats to computer systems from outside include theft, fire, liquids, power failure, vandalism, unauthorised access: from inside the system eavesdropping, hacking, unauthorised access, user error, viruses. NCET advice appears in a leaflet on computer security, extracts of which appear below:

- Try to make sure that your computer equipment is *not* conspicuous from ground-floor windows or located in areas seen by the public. Computers that are not in frequent use or requiring frequent access should be locked away.
- There are a number of measures you can take which will prevent or deter thieves from physically moving the computers, prevent their future sale or stop them being opened.
- Computers owned by the school can be marked with the name and postcode of the school.
- Equipment can also be secured to the desk on which it is used by means of a strong wire or a plate (usually secured with a key) that is fixed on to the computer and the desk. Computers can be kept out-of-hours in a large steel safe, but an alternative for laptops is to disperse them for home use by staff and pupils overnight.
- Computers can be ruined by fire and smoke, which often has a corrosive effect. Water-based extinguishers are not suitable as they will conduct electricity back to the person holding the extinguisher as well as causing more damage to the electronics. Only CO_2 (black), dry powder (blue) or Halon/BCF (green) fire extinguishers are suitable.
- Don't place computers in the vicinity of water and waste pipes. Food and drink should be strictly prohibited in computer rooms.

Protecting data and software

Computer Misuse Act (1990)

This Act protects the authorised data user by enabling prosecution of anyone who accesses a computer without the authority of the recognised user or who deliberately changes the software or data without authority or causes damage. The penalty for infringement is a prison sentence of up to five years and a number of high-profile prosecutions of 'hackers' have taken place.

(NCET, 1996)

- Passwords should be changed regularly, have a minimum of six letters and be made unguessable by including a non-alphabetic letter and avoiding common words and ideas associated with the password owner like a spouse's name or car registration number.
- There must be no possibility of unauthorised access to administrative and financial data, pupil and personnel records.

Copyright, Designs and Patents Act (1988)

This Act and related legislation give protection to computer software, the copyright in which rests with the individual or the company that produced it. A user obtains the right to use the software by buying a licence from a recognised supplier or by obtaining the software as part of package bundled in the sale of the computer. However, the user's rights do not extend to making multiple copies of single-user licensed software for use on a number of computers or for distribution to friends and colleagues.

Special audit software can be obtained to check that your computers or network contain only licenced software. For details contact the Federation Against Software Theft (FAST) on 01628 660377. 'Rationing' software can also be installed on a network to limit the number of concurrent users of a software package to the number of licences you hold for it. In practice, it is usually better for schools to obtain a whole-site licence which may cost no more than a handful of single-user licences.

(NCET, 1996)

Using the Internet

Throughout this book you will see examples of educational material suitable for primary classes which have been obtained through using the Internet. The equivalent of four-and-a-half miles of lorries carrying 22 million thick paperback books represents the movement on the Internet in the USA in just one month. (The growth figures indicate that this probably doubles every six months). Its sheer size — with millions of computers connectable from most countries of the world — means that the information available on all kinds of topics is colossal. This is a rapidly growing area for primary schools and for IT coordinators unfamiliar with 'the net' several aspects of its use are described below, largely taken from NCET's '*Choosing and Using IT Equipment*'.

- Through the Internet your pupils may browse the art collection of the Louvre, download some of the pictures, supplement this with information from the Chicago Art Institute and actualite from *The Guardian*, put it all into a class handout and print it. This is just a part of what access to the Internet can do — and all for the price of a local phone call and a small monthly subscription.
- The Internet is a worldwide computer network which links up thousands of computer networks as well as millions of machines belonging to private individuals.
- There are over one hundred Internet Service Providers (ISPs) in the UK who offer a wide range of online facilities to subscribers, sometimes tailored to particular market sectors and therefore with varying levels of support.
- The Internet provides six main facilities:

  E-mail is electronic mail composed on your computer and transferred, via your ISP, to the Internet.

  Newsgroups are electronic discussion groups, in effect like E-mail but anybody can read the messages and ask a question or add their pearl of wisdom. There are thousands of newsgroups on topics ranging from bee-keeping to baroque art.

  File Transfer Protocol, or FTP, transfers a copy to your computer of any kind of document on which another person has granted access on their computer. You can also attach files to E-mail messages.

  Telnet is the ability to log into a multi-user computer system remotely, for example to use a library catalogue at a distant university.

  Gopher is a menu-based system for accessing and retrieving files, usually academic reports and research papers, across the Internet.

  The World Wide Web is a vast collection of interlinked electronic information pages, now hosted on thousands of web servers worldwide. It is a new, exciting and radical publishing medium. To read web pages you need a software tool known as a browser which fetches and composes the pages on your screen and allows you to pick keywords and hotspots to jump transparently to other web pages (even in a different country) containing linked materials.

- Unfortunately some of the topics on offer are not pleasant and Internet, like high street newsagents and video shops, has its top-shelf section. Several approaches to handling this are possible. The construction of a 'walled garden' as in Research Machines' RMIFL and BT's Campus World, restricts users to seeing only appropriate educational material. More difficult, but of more lasting and wider value, is an effort to educate users about responsibility and ethics. On a recent visit to several Californian schools the author asked about children's access to unsuitable material. In all cases the parents and children had signed a home-school contract — which children agreed not to visit sites displaying unsuitable material. In one school where this had been breached the two boys concerned had been denied further access to computers for the rest of their school career. The news spread quickly!
- Under normal health and safety regulations pupils should not be left unattended, especially in a computer room. Where there is access to the Internet, this is even more important. As IT coordinator, you may still have a responsibility, if a member of your staff leaves pupils unattended long enough for them to download obscene material — or simply does not understand enough about the technology to prevent it. (ACITT, 1996)

It's probably therefore a good idea to subscribe to a managed Internet service, such as RM's Internet for Learning or EDEX's service, and/or to use a program like SurfWatch. At least then you can say you've done as much as you can, as far as physical access is concerned, to prevent the unthinkable from happening. Another aspect of this whole area concerns staff training. The possibility of pupils exploring unsavoury areas when supervised by a teacher who does not know enough to prevent it means that you need to ensure either:

- *that all staff are fully trained in the use of the Internet, or at least trained to the extent that they know when pupils are doing something they shouldn't — highly unlikely to be possible; or*

Negative features of the Net, such as violent, pornographic and racist material, outweigh the benefits for children, writes Tom Conlon, senior lecturer in IT at Moray House Institute, in the *Scottish Educational Review*. He attacks those who equate the Net with the education future and, in the belief that schools cannot afford to be left behind, want Scotland to become '100 per cent wired' to the Net this year.

Mr Conlon is particularly scathing about claims that a child seeking factual information would be better let loose on the Net than sent to a library.

But the Internet is 'neither a library, nor a community, nor a panacea for difficult problems of teaching and learning'. It is of benefit to higher education, and school teachers might be able to cope with its 'chaotic organisation, its absence of quality, its unreliability', but for pupils the negative features loom large and the benefits are much less clear.

Pupils may produce colourful project reports, but 'cutting and pasting is not the same as learning'.

Pickard (1997)

- *non-trained staff are not allowed to cover lessons in rooms where there is access to the Internet — also improbable; or to ensure that Internet access is impossible unless you or another trained member of staff is supervising.*

(ACITT, 1996)

If you are interested in reading more about the Internet, NCET's *Highways for Learning* will give coordinators useful information (and some electronic addresses).

For those who are confused by some of the terms used in publications about communications technology here is an edited quick guide to the most frequently-used terminology concerning the net. (This is however, only 10 per cent of ACITT's list.)

Archie- This is a type of *Internet server* that regularly and automatically indexes the files on a number of Internet servers. Thus, Archie is used to find files on the Internet. Although obviously very useful, it is limited by the fact that it can only search for file names and directory names. It cannot search for keywords or file content.

Baud Rate How quickly a modem sends or receives data. The higher the number the faster the transfer.

BBS Bulletin Board System. An electronic version of the cork bulletin board. Other computers can connect, usually via a modem, to leave messages and/or files and read those left by others.

Bounce When E-mail is returned due to failure to deliver.

Cross post To post the same massage to more than one conference, newsgroup, message area at the same time.

Down Not working, as in 'the BBS is down'.

Down Time While a network is down.

Download The transfer of a file from another, remote, computer to your computer.

E-mail Electronic Mail. A method of sending messages via a computer instead of the usual land-based postal system. One of the most popular and important uses of computer communications.

FAQ Frequently Asked Questions list. This is available in most newsgroups, and '*newbies*' are strongly advised to read it before wading in and asking questions which have already been asked and answered several times. Unless you want to be '*flamed*', of course.

Flame An abusive or personal attack against the poster of the message. A flame is the on-line equivalent of losing your temper!

FTP File Transfer Protocol. This is a means of obtaining (GETting) and uploading (PUTing) files on an Internet site. Once you know the address of the site where the files are kept, you need to access it in a certain way.
As an example, the FTP site of Demon is ftp.demon.co.uk, and this is accessed from the DOS prompt with Demon by typing:
ftp ftp.demon.co.uk.

Gopher The name derives from the words 'go for'. It is a program which enables you to search for files on the Internet, and then obtain the file simply by selecting it from a menu.

HTML This stands for Hypertext Mark-Up Language. By inserting special codes into the text of your WWW pages, you control their appearance and behaviour.

HTTP Hypertext Transfer Protocol, used extensively by World Wide Web. Another of the many Internet protocols.

ISDN Integrated Services Digital Network: an internationally compatible high speed network used for digital services like video conferencing and relatively fast Internet access.

JANET Joint Academic NETwork, one of the original networks: a data communications network linking academic institutions in the UK and connected to similar networks in other European countries and the US.

Login The 'username' or name of your account used for identification purposes.

Netiquette The rules of etiquette for using the Internet.

Netscape A commonly used World Wide Web graphical browser. Has been developed to run on many different platforms e.g. Windows, Amiga, Macintosh.

On-line Connected to an Internet or e–mail service.

POP Post Office Protocol. It is an e–mail protocol used for downloading mail from a server.

Post Send a message to a newsgroup or BBS.

Postmaster The person in charge of the mail over the Internet. Each service provider has a postmaster, who is assisted by programs that, for example, automatically send mail back to the sender if the address is wrong.

Real time When something is going on in real time, it is actually happening at that time. Thus, if you are chatting to someone via your modem in real time they are actually sitting at their computer at the same time as you are sitting at yours.

Surfing Darting from one Internet site to another, just to see what's there.

WWW World Wide Web, a graphical user interface for the Internet.

Connecting to the Internet

PC compatible users

Web browser software runs under Windows and it will need to manipulate large graphics images. So you will need a fast PC such as a Pentium or a 486 with at least 8Mbytes of RAM — do not try to get on to the Internet on older non-windows systems. Your ISP should provide all the software you need and a simple 'install' program to run from Windows to set it all up.

Apple users

The Macintosh needs a proprietary program called MacTCP. Some ISPs bundle this with their Internet software, otherwise you would have to buy it from Apple. You simply install the software and configure the ConfigPPP and MacTCP control panels. Any Mac bought since 1992 should be suitable for Internet use.

Acorn users

The Archimedes has been late aboard Internet, but new faster web browsers are appearing. Call Acorn on 01223 254254 for news.

Modems

- To connect to the Internet you will need a means of connecting to a service provider. Modems convert digital computer data into a series of tones which are sent down the ordinary telephone line whilst another modem, attached to the computer that you wish to connect with anywhere in the world, converts the tones back into computer data at the remote end.
- Whatever your communication needs, you must have a modem and communications software, subscribe to a communications service and pay for telephone use while you are on-line. Some service providers have local 'nodes' so that the user is only charged for connection to the node at local rate. The more nodes the network has, the greater the chances you will have local-rate access.

NCET's Features checklist

- **Standards** — Modems must be approved by the British Approvals Board for Telecommunications (BABT) for connection to the public telephone network. It is an offence to connect and use unapproved equipment. A label with a large green spot shows that the product is approved.
- **Size** — An internal card is dearer but the more expensive often work at a faster speed than an external modem which needs the correct cable (not a printer cable) and connects to the serial port of the computer. PCMCIA cards for notebooks and laptops are now much cheaper. PCMCIA has had compatibility problems and it is wise to buy a notebook bundled with a recommended modem.
- **Connecting leads** — Check whether the modem comes with connecting cables, and if it does, check that they are the correct ones for your computer.
- **Software** — Modems need software to make them work. Many modems come with a communications package included. Free software often implies an old version — with the newer version then offered to you at an 'upgrade' price. When joining the Internet through an Internet Service Provider, many of the providers supply suitable communications software.
- **Fax/Modems** — It is well worth considering a combined unit that will allow you to send both computer data and faxes from a PC. Sending a fax directly from your computer saves time and effort because there is no need to print out a document and then manually feed it into a fax machine. However, if you wish to receive faxes on your computer you will need to keep it switched on all the time or persuade senders to call you beforehand to warn you that they are about to send a fax.

Scanners, OCR and OMR

- Scanners operate by measuring the darkness or colour of lots of points across the surface of the document. This is achieved by shining a light on the document and measuring the amount and colour of the light reflected back by each point.

- Printed documents can be imported into a computer. This may apply to photographs or hand-drawn diagrams — or to text in books or newspapers.
- Optical Mark Reading (OMR) is used to read special computer forms of the type used for multiple-choice examinations, attendance records and questionnaires. Here, OMR equipment detects the presence of handwritten marks on the form and interprets these according to the design of the form.

Data logging

The National Curriculum at Key Stage 2 requires pupils to use information technology to measure external events and record the data from them as part of the development of their IT capability and as part of the science curriculum.

Pupils who use data-logging systems in science experiments have been observed spending much more time talking about what is happening and speculating on what is likely to happen. The fact that they are freed from the chore of manually collecting data makes a contribution to this; but it is the immediacy with which the data is transferred to a graph which makes the difference. An added value is that pupils develop their ability to interpret graphs in a meaningful context.

Data logging requires three main components: an interface for your computer, sensors and suitable software.

Cooling down

A primary class, involved in the NCET Portables Project, was investigating the insulation properties of different materials wrapped around three containers of hot water.

Pupils recorded the heat loss over a two-hour period and were able to see a line graph being updated on their screen every few seconds. This prompted much discussion and speculation about which material was providing the best insulation and how long it might take for the containers to reach room temperature.

This is typical of classroom data-logging activities; freed from the task of reading thermometers and recording data for later conversion to a graph, the pupils were able to focus on what was actually happening, talk about what factors were at work and think how they might improve their investigation.

Running down

With previous experience of using data logging, pupils can be encouraged to use it in their personal projects. One student carried out an experiment to measure the life of a number of batteries.

He wanted to test the claim by a well-known brand of battery that their battery lasted longest.

He connected up a battery to a variable resistor and an ammeter, which in turn was connected to the computer. In this way he was able to run down the battery whilst recording its progress, over a long period of time.

Comparing fabrics

Pupils at a primary school, working on the subject of Britain in the 1940s, tested various fabrics for their suitability as black-out curtains. They devised a fair test using a data-logging interface with a light sensor.

They used a cardboard tube with a light sensor taped with black paper into one end and put the material under test over the end of the tube using a rubber band.

They shone a torch on the material and took a reading of the light level which they displayed on a bar chart on the computer screen. This allowed them to compare the effectiveness of different materials by looking at the heights of the bars.

Data logging interfaces connect to computers and can have sensors plugged into them. They convert the readings which they derive from the sensors into data which the computer can use. Some data loggers have their own memory and power supply and record data without an attached computer.

Programmable toys

For a number of years teachers have exploited toys such as Big Trak (no longer available); ROAMER, PIP and PIXIE to develop children's learning. The keys to the choice between these are:

- What do teachers intend children to learn when using such equipment? What do the children need to know before using the toy — for example that 90° are a right angle/quarter of a turn?
- Is having a rechargeable unit important to you?
- How sophisticated and accurate do you need your unit to be for the intended audience?

Schools who use PIXIE's for Key Stage 1 and Roamers for Key Stage 2 usually achieve progression when the units are exploited for the full range of facilities — but it is not unknown for Y2 and Y6 to be set the same tasks. Hence consider the likely uses before purchase not *post-hoc*.

Pixie is a floor robot small enough to be suitable for table-top use. Its size and simplicity offer many new possibilities for teachers who will welcome the fact that you can assign a small group of children a table-top activity, which is not possible with Roamer and PIP. Pixie is simple with only seven buttons, there are few reception or Year 1 children who will experience any difficulty. In place of numeric values, you simply press the forward or backward buttons once for every multiple of its length. Apart from forward/backward keys, there is a CM (clear memory), which needs to be pressed before any new program of key presses is entered, right and left turn keys, a time (pause) key and a Go key to run the sequence.

Pixie runs from rechargeable batteries that should provide a day's classroom use. What Swallow Systems has done is take the 'how much' out of control, reducing complexity of tasks.

Pixie travels at the same speed as PIP. This means that relative to its size, it is actually completing program steps in half the time it would take PIP or Roamer. For a full report see Drage (1995).

Tamagotchis

This is an already programmed toy giving some scope for investigating the 'what ifs' of computer simulation. Bandai (UK) who import Tamagotchis from Japan claim it '*is a tiny pet from cyberspace who needs your love to survive and grow*'. Certainly once the battery is connected an on-screen egg hatches and provided it is given sufficient attention, fed, played with and disciplined it will grow. Here children, many of whom will have these wristwatch-sized computers, will be familiar with the inputs needed and the consequences of neglect in any particular way. Possibilities exist for comparisons if a record is kept of the characteristics of two or more Tamagotchis who are treated differently. As an introduction to the possibilities of computer simulation, and to making a fair test, IT coordinators might consider a purchase.

Part three Developing policy

Chapter 8 Developing an ICT policy for your school

> *When change is agreed, it is those who are best at doing things the old way who have the most to lose, but by the same token they have the most to offer too.*
>
> Bill Tagg (1996) in *The School in an Information Age.*

Why have an ICT policy?

Key reasons for having a policy document include:
- to guide lesson planning;
- to inform teachers and pupils what is expected of them;
- to identify resource needs; and,
- to inform INSET planning.

A whole school policy for ICT can:
- publicly demonstrate the school's intentions for children's learning with and in ICT;
- help make a case for funding;
- give information on ICT to parents, governors and inspectors;
- provide a framework for individual teacher's planning;
- aid coherence, continuity, progression and shape priorities;
- assist in achieving uniformity and consistency in school decision making by helping to focus the minds of various decision-making groups such as governors, the senior management team, other subject coordinators, toward common aims.

Whether or not your school has the benefit of a written document, it can be argued that a *de-facto* policy exists on the use of ICT in your school. Even if you should find that teachers are entirely free to choose whether or not to use ICT; that children use computers only to play games as a bribe for good behaviour; or that the school's ICT practice merely consists of typing up children's already corrected stories — that amounts to a policy!

The senior management should be impressed by your enthusiasm if you provide a formal written policy that should improve the use of the computers in your school.

If a policy document exists then you have a starting point to compare practice and policy and something to guide discussions with staff. If not, or if the policy bears no relation to reality, then sooner or later you will need to begin the process of working with your teacher colleagues to create one which does.

The only point of a written whole school policy for ICT is that it is owned by the whole staff, describes what is actually happening in the classroom and gives some indication of the direction the school is going with regard to the use of computers and other ICT equipment. If in its construction teachers become a little more aware about how other teachers are using computers, which computer skills are being developed in each part of the school, and which programs are being used, then a more coherent approach may well evolve without you having to do very much at all. A clearer understanding of a progression in ICT skills may grow amongst staff through open discussion, and more and less appropriate uses of the school's computers may be debated without you ever having to declare your hand.

A whole school policy for ICT can publicly demonstrate the school's intentions for children's learning with and in ICT. It is the school's chance to say to those who pay for these resources, those whose children use them and the community at large which has great expectations in their use *'This is what we believe'; 'This is what we intend to do'; 'This is how we see your children developing ICT capability whilst they are with us'*. This is your opportunity to make clear that we are about *'computing for education'* rather than *'education about computing'*. We can declare that we believe the useful role of computers in the early years is as a medium for social interaction both within and between schools and encourage the development of language through the sharing of enjoyable activities with peers and adults — if that's what we do think — which might dispel some of the more reactionary thinking prevalent in some quarters.

The policy document will need to show the mechanisms in place that the school has to:

- stay informed of developments, both technical and curricular;
- develop the curriculum in the light of those changes;
- resource any subsequent needs;
- keep staff skills up-to-date.

After Smith (1996)

Carefully researched arguments can help make a case for irreducible future funding, as the policy should show how the school is planning for future ICT developments. ICT has a unique place in the work of primary schools. Technology will continue to develop at an increasing rate and new curriculum applications will continually emerge. Future funding will need to be earmarked to enable the school to be aware of those developments.

A well defined and readable document should give useful information on ICT to parents, governors and inspectors. What do parents really want to know? Many parents will be content with a general outline of the types of application with which their children will become increasingly familiar while moving through the school. Some may well wish to know the hardware platforms and specific program which you will be using in order to make home purchases. Others may wish to be informed about the protected Internet environment you use. A parents' cybercafé one evening a week, one term a year, staffed on a rota basis is well used in some primary schools to inform parents.

Parents will expect you to ensure that the policy is implemented and governors, too, will want accurate information, particularly in relation to the effectiveness of the resource allocation as it is spent to build up equipment in the school. They may also be interested in the evaluations you make about the effectiveness of your spending decisions.

Inspectors are dealt with in Part 4 but suffice to say here that as well as the information above they would expect to see in your policy some detail about the way in which the policy is monitored and estimates made of the quality of work in this area.

The process of the policy's development may:

- help participants understand teaching and learning strategies with ICT employed by other staff;
- help create a team spirit in making public the school's goals;
- offer a means of evaluation of the ICT work being planned;
- help clarify functions and responsibilities of staff, and;
- help new staff to settle in.

Along with an appropriate scheme of work, your ICT document should provide a useful framework for individual teacher's planning. The test of a good policy document is how frequently it is referred to in the course of planning a lesson, sequence of lessons or in medium-term planning. Is your school's document left in the drawer and only brought out on high days, holidays and *OFSTED* days? Considering the effort which is invested in these few sheets of paper surely it should be the focus of attention for some of the time? When completed your document should aid coherence, continuity, progression and shape priorities amongst staff. It should help teachers to speak to each other about their work using information and communications technology, which may help them to understand how their own contribution to developing children's capability fits in with the efforts of others and just how much attention needs to be paid to children's work with computers.

The end result should assist in achieving uniformity and consistency in school decision-making by helping to focus the minds of various decision-making groups such as governors, the senior management team, and other subject coordinators, toward common aims.

A host of factors can help or hinder the development of ICT in any school. The attitude of the head, influential governors, the way any excess money is allocated and, when necessary, where the cuts should fall. Having an agreed policy document that has been discussed by staff and governors and shown to parents can help to influence key decision-making groups towards your aims and objectives or at least make them feel they will have a fight on their hands if they choose to wield the axe in your direction. ICT is the most cross-curricular of subjects, so if we want coordinators from the core and foundation subjects to help us to promote ICT through their subjects we shall need to have a clear plan laid before them so that they can incorporate our strategies and objectives where appropriate. Thus an agreed plan for ICT that is at the start of the development cycle can be a great advantage.

The process in which you have been involved may help colleagues to understand teaching and learning strategies with ICT employed by other staff. A democratic forum where best practice is also rehearsed and the discussion on the ways in which ICT is practised by members of staff in various parts of the school should not only provide you with a better policy but also help teachers to learn from one another. Indeed your work in this area might have contributed to the creation of a greater team spirit in making public the school's goals and providing a forum whereby teachers can act as professional critical friends.

The discussions may have helped to clarify functions and responsibilities of different members of staff. Together you may detail what each of your roles in this process will be.

Allocation of roles and responsibilities in an ICT-effective school						
Task	SMT	Head	IT Coord	All staff	Contract out	Others
Organize and manage groups to write ICT policy						
Alert others to local ICT support services						
Assist in the design of ICT development plans						
Responsible for ordering and distributing ICT equipment around the school						
Create opportunities for teacher training and development in school						
Ensure equality of opportunity with ICT						
Identity needs and formulate policies for ICT across the curriculum						
Plan and provide ICT INSET for other teachers						
Keep abreast of current philosophies in the use of ICT						
Alert others to the nature of IT capability as defined in the NC						
Alert others to the uses of ICT as a tool to enhance learning						
Attend all the courses offered by the LEA						
Compile and produce timetables for ICT equipment						
Diagnose equipment faults (simple)						
Oversee and ensure the batanced delivery of ICT across the curriculum						
Evaluate classroom practice involving the use of ICT						
Inform other staff of good, bad and interesting practice using ICT						
Keep a list of hardware and software available in school						
Manage and maintain hard disks on all machines						
Monitor and assess the uses of ICT made by pupils						
Negotiate the purchase of site licences for key places of software						
Provide classroom based ICT support for staff in all cuniculum areas						
Recommend ICT activities for different curriculum situations						
Recommend appropriate software for pupil and teacher needs						
Regularly discuss ICT provision with Head and subject coordinators						
Repair computer equipment (simple)						
Represent the school at LEA meetings for ICT coordinators						
Set up displays showing a range and uses of ICT in school						
Liaise cross-phase to ensure continuity of experience in ICT						
Build and program concept keyboard overlays for all staff						
Deliver ICT skills to all pupils in the school						
Keep records of pupils' progress through levels of attainment in ICT						
Prepare reports on individual pupils' progress in ICT						
Alert others to the uses and importance of ICT in society at large						
Manage the school information system, support and train admin. staff						
Produce school publications using desk-top publishing equipment						
Diagnose equipment faults (complex)						
Make and repair cables for computer equipment						
Repair computer equipment (complex)						
Supervise the IT technician (joke)						

(Adapted from Clemson,. 1996, *The Primary Core Curriculum*, edited by Coulby and Ward, Cassell Education)

The allocation of roles will depend on your school situation, but the discussion which leads to decisions about such an allocation may well be to the advantage of the IT coordinator. Many heads and other staff will not be aware of the complexities and sheer volume of the role. It might well lead to discussions of time allocation to match the extent of the tasks it is agreed that you should carry out. Working together to create or revise the policy document may offer a means of evaluation of the ICT work being planned. How does it match up to your policy's ideals? It may also help new staff to settle in and reveal the role they play in the processes in your school. You might wish to ask recently arrived teachers whether any of the documents they were given helped them in their first terms? How did the ICT policy fare by comparison with the others?

An action plan to develop your school's ICT policy

1 Consult with colleagues
2 Draft a scheme of work
3 Organise the resources
4 Try out the scheme in action
5 Review and revise

You will need to go through several stages in order to arrive at a policy document and scheme of work which will serve the purposes set out in the tinted box.

The process outlined here may take several months, but it is likely to take much longer. The change process may develop its own momentum and may keep itself going, although it is more likely to require continual re-emphasis. Coordinators must accept that teachers' initial enthusiasm may be short-lived when they discover the full implications of the change.

It will be useful to identify stages in the progression towards and through the change to an acceptable policy document.

Suggestion

Consider outside influences. Make sure that if there is advice from QCA or DfEE that you have read it. Make contact with a local adviser, advisory teacher, school, college or university where advice may be available. Take note of any courses which might help you or your colleagues. Enquire about any national association for teachers of your subject. Do they have a primary section? Do they have local meetings? How does the local community fit in? Are there people within your community with interest or expertise? Parents are bound to be interested at some point. How will they hear about the changes you propose? Make sure that you lay plans to manage this information. What involvement of parents might be considered?

Assess the current policy
Build the need for change
Consult the staff and plan together
Draft a document and discuss

Each stage isn't quite as easy as ABC as we shall see. Each is clarified and strategies are considered below.

Assess the current policy

It is important for you to know the school's position and what factors will influence it from the outside. You will need to be open about what you are doing and to beware of raising the profile of ICT until you are ready. We all react badly to having issues forced upon us!

Gather opinion about the policy document and how well it reflects the quality and extent of children's work in ICT across each curriculum area. Find out how policy documents have been developed in the past. How have colleagues previously responded to change?

Build the need

Establish a file where you keep:

- your notes;
- relevant documents;
- perhaps a diary.

This will help you to show development and progress over time and to demonstrate your success. Talk to the headteacher in order to:

- determine ICT's current priority within the school development plan;
- establish a professional dialogue between you and the headteacher;
- register your interest and commitment;
- negotiate the next step;
- emphasise the need;
- formulate a rationale and targets for your work.

Suggestion

- Show positive results through your own practice.
- Make sure you can spell out how it will benefit the children.
- Identify work already going on in many classrooms.
- Demonstrate how it will support other areas of the curriculum.
- Explain that it is a legal requirement.

It will also be helpful to rehearse your thoughts and to think about possible pitfalls. These may be presented to you in an attempt to divert you or hinder your progress by any member of staff.

- 'the staff have had too much thrown at them recently'
- 'we've not got the time'
- 'we lack the resources'
- 'Mrs Black tried this some years ago and it didn't work then'
- 'do you do this yourself?'
- 'The Internet contains pornography . . .'
- 'our children can't cope with . . .'
- 'we've got this in hand already, don't you bother to stir up . . .'

In order to deal with these you must be clear about why you are promoting the development or change. Your arguments need to be reasonable and practical (see left-hand column).

Here are some examples that you may use. It is important to be specific.

- 'The lower juniors teachers are trying to teach LOGO and so using the Roamer within the early years programme will develop vital skills.'
- 'This Website allows maths skills and understanding to be practically used.'
- 'History and science can be developed together when we look at houses of long ago in the Landmarks programmes.'
- 'Children are already interested in using computers and using these downloaded pictures will help in teaching geography.'

So far you have been gathering information. You are now ready to draw up your plan of action.

Construct a plan of action to support the development of a policy

It is important that you start to think in terms of a plan of action for developing the ICT policy. This is not a blue-print to be followed by the letter but an agenda which takes account of constraints on development and is realistic about time required

Suggestion

To get every teacher to include the appropriate use of computers to support class topics.

To encourage a wider range of presentation of reports though word processing in every class.

To develop links with other classes of children in the USA and students in India.

Integrating aspects of IT into the school's history policy.

Development of simple control technology in Y5 and Y6 to capitalise on cross-curricular links through project work.

for stages to be implemented. It will require constant reappraisal.

In order to write this plan try to write a statement in one simple sentence that will act as an aim.

For those unfamiliar with this process a tip is to write down all the relevant words and phrases and then try to pare them down to one statement. The next step will be to jot down lots of ways that your aims might be realised. Divide up your list and say whether these can realistically be achieved, tackled or addressed in the long, medium or short term (you can decide what is meant by short term). This should put you in a position to make some clear statements of intent and a possible order in which to tackle them. This has to be seen as a working agenda and can only be presented as your personal thinking so far. In later stages you will allow others to influence your thinking, and the course of events. This may be the mechanism by which you hand over ownership of the process to your colleagues.

So far we have described a simple plan of action. Firstly we establish where we are, then determine where we want to be and then we work out a possible route from the former to the latter, recognising that ultimately we may need to diverge.

Doing it

Who can help us? How can we help ourselves? How will we know when we get there?

1 Where are we now?
2 Where do we want to get to?
3 How will we get there?

Write a statement of intent with colleagues.

> Every child at Falmer Street Primary School is entitled to an ICT curriculum which is varied, challenging and inspiring, and one which enables each individual to fulfil her or his potential to the highest possible standard and develop skills, knowledge and attitudes to the benefit of all.

This will remind you of your distant aims even when absorbed by little local difficulties. Stating your intentions in black and white will have an effect. The process of writing itself will act as a catalyst. It will also mean that views do come out into the open, some may be critical, so be prepared. It may be profitable to refer to it as a draft statement. Your aim should be to produce a simple, accessible, jargon-free, description of practice in school. Give some thought to the methods of establishing agreement about general aims and intent (is agreement only skin deep?).

Consider the desired outcomes over time. Here are some developed by the Essex IT advisory team and colleagues which examine in turn outcomes for parents, teachers, and managers.

In a school developing the effective use of IT one might expect that:

- parents will recognise the benefits of using IT as part of children's education;
- parents see the IT experiences their child gains at home being encouraged and developed in school;
- teachers use IT effectively;
- teachers are receiving appropriate training and updating of their skills;
- teachers use IT in their lesson planning and preparation;
- teachers network with colleagues in other institutions to keep up to date and obtain resources;
- teachers consider the role of IT as a resource for differentiation;
- managers are prepared for continuing change;
- managers make effective use of IT in administration;
- managers monitor the use of new technology.

This group went on to describe the expected outcomes for pupils who had attended such a school.

Knowledge and understanding

- Understand that IT can be used to solve problems in a range of contexts
- Know when to use a particular IT toll in the solution of a problem
- Know the limitations of IT and when not to use it
- Begin to understand the impact of new technology on society

Skills

- Handle hardware with increasing confidence
- Continue to develop skills in the use of software
- Apply these skills to a wider range of contexts

Personal development

- Show confidence and autonomy when using new technology
- Become purposeful and discerning users
- Be able to reflect on their work and on the work of others

Using this rationale the next chapter presents a prototype policy ready for adoption and development in any primary school.

Chapter 9 A prototype policy

> *The school policy should reflect actual practice, stating the current procedures for making the IT curriculum work effectively. The document will have been accepted by senior management and the governing body. If the draft documents presented are not acceptable, the draft will need revision. If it is in the policy, it should be happening.*
>
> *The Information Technology Handbook* (Essex County Council, 1996)

The seven sections of the prototype policy presented here are offered to give you a skeleton on which to hang your own ideas and suggestions. I have used this over a number of years to stimulate discussion amongst staff in primary schools who are working towards a policy for ICT. Most areas will need discussion and agreement with your own staff to be meaningful but it is sometimes useful to have a starting document, if only to give you all something to knock down. A general heading in each section is followed by suggestions in italics for schools to modify as they think best fits their own situation. Many of these statements come from primary schools' IT policy documents given to the author over a number of years, and others from suggestions within Heather Govier's policy published in MAPE in 1994 and others derived from Essex Council's *Information Technology Handbook*, and IT policies from Trafford LEA. The document cannot be used as a whole because many of the example statements are contradictory.

Policy for the use of information and communications technology at Falmer Street Primary School

1. Introduction

1.1. What do we mean by ICT (Information and Communications Technology)?

The work children do in ICT (Information and Communications Technology) may be with computers, programmable robots, calculators, video cameras, the Internet and/or tape recorders. This document is a statement of our aims, strategies and intentions in this area, but largely centres on the use of computers.

IT (Information Technology) is the term used to cover a number of artefacts and systems which retrieve data electronically. It can mean tape and video recorders, calculators and robots but its major use at Falmer Primary School is in the use of computers. ICT is similar to IT but emphasises the communication aspect of the technology.

Information technology capability is characterised by an ability to use effectively ICT tools and information sources to analyse, process and present information, and to model, measure and control external events.

1.2. Why ICT?

Staff at Falmer Street County Primary believe that it is important that children's studies be enhanced by the use of computer technology as its use is widespread throughout the world today and is likely to become more so before our children mature and leave school.

All children will be encouraged to develop positive attitudes towards information and communications technology. They will be helped to develop confidence and enjoyment in, and an understanding of, the potential of computer applications including e-mail and the World Wide Web.

Through a variety of experiences we aim for each child to develop skills in the following areas:

- *communicating ideas through words, pictures and sounds entering, storing and classifying information;*

- *accessing and obtaining information (e.g. from a CD ROM) giving signals and commands.*

We believe that teaching and learning can be improved by the appropriate use of computers. Schools are inspected by OFSTED on the quality of their provision, teaching and learning of information technology.

Pupils should be given opportunities, where appropriate, to develop and apply their information technology capability in their study of each subject in the National Curriculum (Statutory Orders).

1.3. Statement of aims
This should be a general statement of the school's agreed intent in this area, which is suitable for teachers, school governors, the LEA and OFSTED inspectors. It needs to be based on National Curriculum requirements and declare that every child should have access to learning in IT and that the school is dedicated to achievement in this area. The statement should reflect the school's ethos and overall aims.

Children at Falmer Street Primary School are entitled to gain access to the National Grid for Learning.

Falmer St Primary School's approach to teaching and learning ICT is to use 'computing for education' rather than provide 'education about computing'.

It is our intention that our children will experience a wide range of ICT applications, enjoy using computers and grow in confidence and competence as they progress through the school.

ICT will be used to support each area of the curriculum. Computer technology can both support and enhance the curriculum through the application of databases, word processing, control and simulations and the use of communications technology.

At Falmer St we see the use of ICT as one way in which children's communication skills can be developed through letter writing, group work creating class newsletters, group problem solving, communicating with children in distant places by e-mail, retrieving information via the Internet, researching and reporting searches of CD ROM encyclopaedia.

Any or none of the above statements may describe your own position but this vital opening section must be drawn up jointly by the head teacher and coordinator and agreed by staff and governors before detailed work on guidelines and the rest of the policy can begin in earnest.

1.4. How the policy has been prepared or what state it is in at present

ICT is a priority on the school development plan for 1998/90. This document is a position statement drawn up by the co-ordinator in preparation for staff discussion during this period.

This is a draft document prepared by the coordinator with a view to informing discussion at the staff training day scheduled for Spring 1999.

1.5. What (if it is not clear already) is the purpose of this document?

This policy and scheme of work is intended to inform teachers' day to day planning and should be frequently referred to in forecasts.

The purpose of this document is to inform staff, pupils and governors what is expected of them if we are to make best use of and achieve the highest quality standards in ICT.

At this point the contents of the rest of the document might be listed with page numbers or readers otherwise signposted through the document.

2. Implementation

2.1. Towards achieving policy aims

Experiences the school intends to give children in order to achieve the above policy aims and objectives should appear here. This may take the form of an interpretation of the NC Programmes of Study and Attainment Targets that takes into account the circumstances of your school. This section is not the scheme of work itself but the document does require sufficient detail to ensure continuity of approach and progression of work throughout the school.

As a school we have an ICT focus each term namely:
Autumn — Word processing
Spring — Control and monitoring
Summer — Data handling

By Year 4 children will have been introduced to the use of CD ROMs and will regularly be required to extract and print out information of personal interest or in connection with the class topic.

Children's experiences of information and communications technology should incorporate:

- *word processing for a variety of purposes;*
- *using communications packages;*
- *data handling;*
- *use of a concept keyboard (at Key Stage 1);*
- *use of programmable toys and household devices such as tape recorders;*
- *opportunities to work independently and co-operatively;*
- *use of IT based models and simulations.*

Specific skills and experiences to be taught in each class are detailed in the scheme of work which forms part of this policy. Computer use is carefully managed so that all pupils are given equal access opportunities. Each child uses a computer at least once a week.

The emphasis in our teaching with Information Technology is on the use of computers as tools to support learning. Thus all pupils are made familiar with basic aspects of disc and printer management and efficient use of the keyboard and mouse. Word processing is the application most widely used. Throughout the school most activities using ICT are allied to other work carried out away from the computer. As pupils progress through the school they are given increasing control of their use of ICT, gaining growing independence in their use of ICT as a tool appropriate to any given activity and in their choice of software required.

Curriculum maps, software maps and definite plans can help to ensure that the policy is adhered to rather than vague promises.

2.2. Resources
The equipment and materials to which children will have access (are entitled to) by means of this policy.

Every child will have experience of using a programmable robot and/or turtle linked to LOGO by the time they reach Year 4.

Calculators are available in all classrooms.

Each class has an A3000 computer and two PCs with CD ROMs are housed in the library for research purposes. One is connected to the Internet, and communicators are protected from unsuitable material by a commercial firewall.

A suite of computers in the library are networked and linked to the Internet and all children will have an e-mail address and access to the World Wide Web.

2.3. Social and cross-curricular outcomes
This may be a suitable point to remind readers that gaining knowledge is not the only outcome of the teaching process.

By use of communications technology children will be encouraged to develop their understanding of and empathy with children from other parts of the world.

Some uses of ICT are designed to enhance cooperative group work and develop problem solving strategies. Use of the Roamer, in particular, can involve groups of children in lively discussion.

ICT is a means for developing group work, autonomy and confidence and encouraging the consideration of the limitations of the process, and a reflection of work.

2.4. Teaching styles
There is also a place for using the construction of this document in helping to gain agreement between staff on the methods which will be used to promote learning in classes. If this can be done it may be recorded at this point in your policy document. This will help to remindeveryone what they agreed.

All classrooms are equipped with calculators and a computer. It is our aim that children should work on a computer regularly. Children may be required to work individually, in pairs or in small groups according to the nature or activity of the task.

Homework is not used to support ICT work as access to home computers is very variable.

In many homes the quality and level of ICT resources outstrip those available in school. Teachers will gauge the ICT experience of their pupils and planning will take account of ICT resources available at home.

The IT coordinator is responsible both for the storing of master disks and the distribution of software to appropriate classes. A variety of Website addresses are listed at the back of this policy document. A 'live' storage file is to be kept of favourite sites and useful addresses will be listed there.

Subject coordinators have chosen a wide range of software to support teaching and learning in each subject for all age ranges. Subject specific disks are kept by the appropriate coordinator.

Children working with programmable robots, such as the ROAMER, will normally be engaged in problem solving activities in groups outside the classroom or elsewhere.

Work in ICT is frequently group work although computers are sometimes used by individuals for word processing or for the practice of basic skills. IT is rarely used for class teaching. Groups of pupils using ICT vary in size from pairs (most common) to groups of 6/8 (for programs where discussion is paramount) and

- *are usually of matched ability as this makes for more equal interaction;*
- *may occasionally be of mixed ability to enable more competent children to help those less so (for example in word processing activities in the early years);*
- *are usually of matched gender in order to avoid the commonly experienced marginalisation of girls as boys monopolise the equipment;*
- *may be involved in teaching one another through a rolling program (for example when introducing a new piece of software).*

There is no specialist teaching in ICT, its use is integrated into normal classroom work.

Specially trained parents are used in most classrooms to provide support for ICT activities.

Pupils who are eager and interested in the use of ICT are used in many classrooms to set up equipment and as 'experts' in various applications — able to advise peers if they encounter problems. Year 6 pupils also act as monitors for infant classes.

2.5. Equal opportunities and multiculturalism
Your school's equal opportunities statement and any subject specific multicultural issues might appear at this point.

At Falmer Street Primary School we believe all our children are entitled to benefit from access to a curriculum which takes account of unequal starting points. Therefore certain pupils will have enhanced access to the information and communications activities.

All children regardless of race, gender, intellectual and physical ability . . . will be given equal access to work and equipment. Classroom management will take account of such issues, and ICT materials free from bias will be positively sought.

Pupils with special needs have the same ICT entitlement as all other pupils and are offered the same curriculum. In addition, particular applications of ICT are used for pupils with difficulties in learning, who need to be motivated to practise basic skills regularly and intensively, and thus benefit from the use of programs in which skills practise is set in the context of a motivating game. Certain pupils with physical or communication handicaps who have their own specially adapted machines for use in communication and across the curriculum, pupils of high ability who may be extended through the use of programs which offer challenge and opportunities for investigation, are given special entitlement.

2.6. Roles and responsibilities

The names and roles of persons responsible for overseeing or coordinating the implementation of the policy need to be recorded here along with the various responsibilities of head and class teachers with regard to this.

The head teacher will organise the development of the policy; coordinate INSET to support policy aims; ensure the balanced delivery of ICT across the curriculum; monitor the implementation of the scheme of work; evaluate classroom practice in the use of ICT and regularly disseminate aspects of good practice to staff . . .

The IT coordinator will alert other teachers to local support and courses; run incidental Inset; order and distribute software, recommend ICT activities wherever possible . . .

Class teachers will be responsible for reading the ICT policy document and implementing it in their classrooms. When needing help or advice they will ask the coordinator rather than deny children their entitlements. They will use the scheme of work in all levels of planning and make sure that each child has a plastic wallet in which to keep both record sheets and printouts. Teachers will check that they have, and are familiar with, the software necessary to implement their part of the curriculum as detailed in the school software map.

2.7. Methods for monitoring children's progress and continuity

All teachers plan for the use of information and communications technology in their own classes. A termly staff meeting is used to discuss the use being made of ICT across the curriculum and ensure consistency of approach and of standards. We are particularly keen that children will be able to benefit from the National Grid for Learning. Half termly work plans (including detailed lesson plans) which are drawn up by individual teachers and monitored by the head teacher, all include proposals for integrated ICT use.

Software throughout the school has been carefully mapped out to ensure that pupils' experience of ICT is continuous and progressive.

The information technology coordinator will:

- *take the lead in policy development and the integration of ICT into schemes of work designed to ensure progression and continuity in pupil's experience of ICT throughout the school;*
- *support colleagues in their efforts to include ICT in their development of detailed work plans, in their implementation of those schemes of work and in assessment and record-keeping activities;*
- *monitor children's progress in ICT and advise the headteacher on action needed take responsibility for the purchase and organisation of central resources for ICT;*
- *provide technical support to colleagues in their use of ICT in the classroom and pass on information to colleagues as appropriate.*

Who is responsible for seeing that the agreed practices are being carried out in all classes? Who is to ensure children's entitlement? It may be covered above but still might need saying so here. How will this be done?

3. Schemes of work

Whole-school, or Key Stage schemes of work may be included here or as a separate document. This should fit in with everyone else's method of handling such matters.

You might wish to begin by considering the machine handling skills to be developed at certain times in children's careers.

3.1. Developing machine-handling skills

machine-handling skills in Key Stage 1 and Key Stage 2							
	Nur Rec	Y1	Y2	Y3	Y4	Y5	Y6
Turning on the machine							
Loading a disk							
Starting a program							
Printing a file							
Switching/logging off							
Taking care of disks							
Mouse skills							
Return/enter key							
Saving to disk — same disk							
Recovering from disk — same disk							
Operating the printer							
Selecting appropriate software							
Saving to disk — work disk							
Recovering from disk — work disk							
Using integrated programs							
Formatting a disk							
Copying disks							
Downloading files							
Printing out e-mail messages							
Copying files							

(from Clemson, 1996, *The Primary Core Curriculum*, edited by Coulby and Ward, Cassell Education)

3.2. An overview from the National Curriculum for Key Stage 1:

Pupils should be given opportunities to:

1 *use a variety of IT equipment and software including microcomputers and various keyboards, to carry out a variety of functions in a range of contexts;*

2 *explore the use of computer systems and control technology in everyday life;*

3 *examine and discuss their experiences of IT, and look at the use of IT in the outside world.*

Pupils should be taught to use computers to:

Communicate and handle information;

1 *generate and communicate their ideas in different forms using text, tables, pictures and sound;*

2 *enter and store information;*

3 *retrieve, process and display information that has been stored.*

Control and model

1 *recognise that control is integral to many everyday devices;*

2 *give direct signals or commands that produce a variety of outcomes, and describe the effects of their actions;*

3 *use IT based models and simulations to explore aspects of real and imaginary situations.*

3.3. ICT Skills at KS1 might be listed here.

3.3.1. Communicating information

As part of their KS1 experiences children will be taught to:

- *use the mouse for a variety of purposes;*
- *manipulate the pointer using the mouse e.g. 'click and drag' to make a picture;*
- *press a concept keyboard to make the computer do something;*
- *click the select button to make choices;*
- *join with the class in exploring CD ROMs on topics of interest;*
- *click the middle button to bring up a menu;*
- *copy or type their own name for use as a label;*
- *copy or write a sentence;*
- *with help find Webpages of interest such as the Disney Website and print out topics of interest;*
- *select a font;*
- *change the size of a font;*

- *write something about a picture that has been put on the page;*
- *use capital letters and full stops in their writing;*
- *load previously saved work to change it;*
- *work in a small group to produce a piece of writing;*
- *click and drag a picture onto their writing;*
- *print their work using the print button;*
- *manipulate 'My World' screens;*
- *add their own text to 'My World' screens;*
- *use the talking books and develop their skills in turning pages and manipulating pictures.*

3.3.2. Handling information

As part of their KS1 experiences children will be taught to . . .

- *enter items into a program like Pictogram to produce a simple picture, for example, how we travel to school;*
- *process and display information;*
- *change the data by adding or deleting items;*
- *use a graphing program like Dataplot which uses automatic scaling;*
- *decide which is the best graph style for their data;*
- *print out a graph;*
- *change an incorrect entry.*

3.3.3. Controlling and modelling

As part of their Key Stage 1 experiences children will be taught to . . .

- *recognise how everyday toys and devices (such as robots and automatic doors), respond to signals and switches;*
- *use the tape recorder to stop and start a story or music;*
- *use the control buttons to make a robotic device (Roamer) do something;*
- *give instructions to move the robot in any predetermined direction;*
- *use repeat to make something happen more than once;*
- *use adventure programs such as 'Granny's Garden' and 'Teddy Bear's Picnic' to explore imaginary situations;*
- *use Microworld to place and move objects around the house and garden;*
- *use the CD in a variety of ways e.g. Maximania;*

- *use a range of programs in connection with other work e.g. My World.*

3.4. ICT skills at Key Stage 2

The scheme of work should detail how the capabilities developed earlier are built upon at Key Stage 2. The National Curriculum requirements may be listed here.

3.4.1. Communicating information

As part of their KS2 experiences children will be taught to . . .

- *use word processing tools, e.g. spellchecker, underline;*
- *change font, colour and size of text;*
- *work in a small group to produce a report or poster;*
- *load previously saved work to change and improve it, for example edit and redraft a piece of work to improve punctuation and paragraphs;*
- *import pictures or borders to a piece of writing and select suitable size and position for them;*
- *read and write e-mails and where appropriate enter information onto a communal Web homepage*
- *produce labels for own books or displays;*
- *move towards a greater independence in their use of programs, for instance add their own text to My World screens;*
- *create and play a tune;*
- *create a design or logo to use as a letterhead or emblem.*

3.4.2. Handling information

As part of their Key Stage 2 experiences children will be taught to . . .

- *enter items into a graphing program to produce pictorial information;*
- *convert different types of information into graphs or pictograms;*
- *sort the data by numbers or words and discuss how this alters the graph;*
- *edit and amend the data to correct a wrong entry;*
- *select the most appropriate type of graph for the data they have entered and the purposes of the activity;*
- *use a CD ROM and the Internet to investigate data about a topic.*

3.4.3. Controlling, monitoring and modelling

As part of their KS2 experiences children will be taught to . . .

- *control a screen turtle around a pre-determined course;*
- *write a simple procedure in LOGO for drawing a shape;*

- *experiment with repeat patterns;*
- *link a series of commands together to form a procedure;*
- *understand that procedures have names and can be saved on disc;*
- *edit a procedure;*
- *use modelling programs to explore and investigate computer based representations of situations, for example Sim City, which would be impossible to represent in any other way;*
- *use a simulation of an archaeological exploration to discover and identify artefacts of a particular era;*
- *use adventure games to develop problem solving skills;*
- *use increasingly challenging programs which provide a context for work already going on in the classroom.*

3.5.
Themes or topics may be used as the basis for planning by year groups. This represents long term planning from which individual teachers will create forward, medium-and then short-term work plans. Whatever the method is in your school it is a good idea to state it here — then everyone knows where they stand.

Subject specific lessons form only the minority of work here at Falmer Street Primary and ICT contributes to cross-curricular study in a variety of ways. Dorling Kindersley CD ROMs on many topics are shared with St Stephen's Primary and can be loaned for periods up to a term. Please see the IT coordinator.

As each year group plans the topics for each half term. The IT coordinator may be approached to recommend specific software or Website addresses to support study in that area. Library loan services may be accessed and, provided sufficient notice is given, it may be possible to purchase products which have a wider application from funds put aside for that purpose.

3.6.
The way ICT will be used to support learning with cross curricular links.

Children will be introduced to the use of databases to support their work in geography in Year 5.

Three different word processing packages are used to help children practise the process of writing. Each package has been chosen to give children access to more sophisticated features as they progress though the school.

3.7.
A synopsis of work covered in the first year of the high school may be usefully included here.

4. Assessment and recording of pupils' progress

List here the purposes of assessment and uses to which records of children's achievement will be put.

Formative assessment is used to guide the progress of individual pupils in their use of ICT. It involves identifying each child's progress, determining what each child has learned and what, therefore, should be the next stage in his/her learning. Formative assessment is mostly carried out informally by teachers in the course of their teaching. Suitable tasks for assessment of ICT work include small group discussions, perhaps in the context of a practical task, specific ICT assignments for individual pupils.

4.1.
Agreed methods of record-keeping and times at which such assessments will be made.

Teachers' records of children's experiences are kept in annotated forecast books.

Individual discussions in which children are encouraged to appraise their own work and progress will be recorded.

Example sheets of work in ICT are kept systematically throughout the year. A summative record is compiled each summer to pass to the next teacher.

Records of progress in information technology are kept for each child and contain a termly record of progress in each strand. A portfolio of work is compiled, dated and annotated with teacher comments and containing one item for each half term which shows achievement and progress.

Reporting to parents is done on a termly basis through interviews and annually through a written report. Reporting on ICT use will focus on each child's ability to use a computer with confidence and competence across a variety of applications.

Records of the children's experiences and skills will be kept. These will be in the form of simple child-centred record of achievement sheets and a file containing several pieces of work in the form of 'print outs' annotated as to the date and the program used. As new work is placed in the file old work of the same type may be sent home. Teachers will also be required to keep records to ensure children have regular and varied ICT experiences and are developing their skills (see Figure 9.1).

This section should not be at variance with the school's assessment and recording policy and certainly not at odds

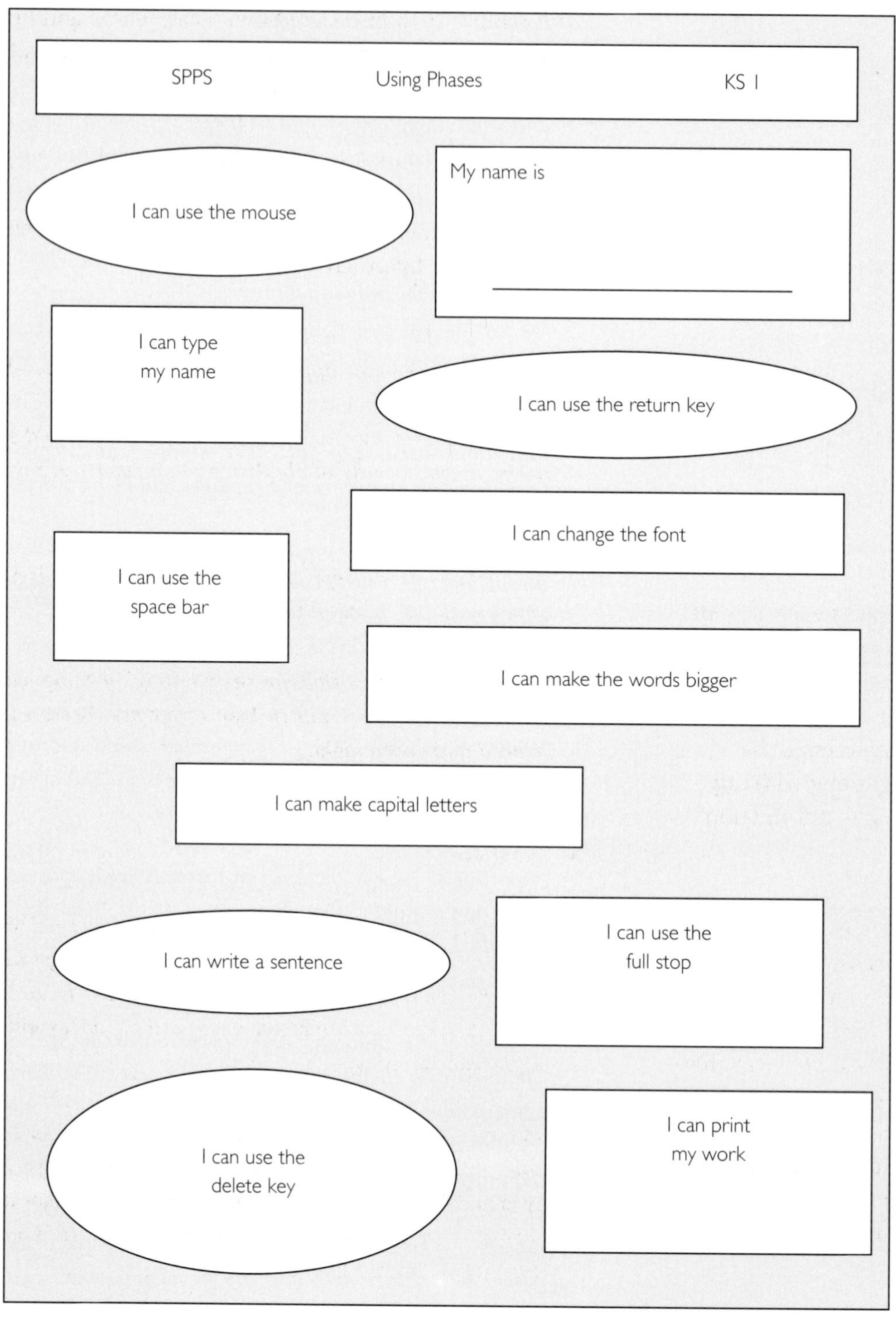
SPPS Using Phases KS 1

My name is ____________

I can use the mouse

I can type my name

I can use the return key

I can change the font

I can use the space bar

I can make the words bigger

I can make capital letters

I can write a sentence

I can use the full stop

I can use the delete key

I can print my work

FIG 9.1
Children's own record at KS1

(Seymour Park Primary School)

with reality! It should state how, what, where and how often. It might even say why records are kept, what the real purpose of plotting pupils' progress is in your school.

How do you report progress to parents?

It may be desirable to demonstrate in the policy document what is meant by progression.

IT progression will be demonstrated by children carrying out more complex tasks, applying more advanced skills, becoming more independent and confident using ICT, and by using more sophisticated software. For this to happen and good progress to be made, records of children's attainment will need to be accurate and up to date.

4.2.
The location of examples of children's work which exemplifies levels of attainment and progression between them might be stated here along with any other germane information.

Exemplar files are kept in the staff room and children's individual records stored in the office.

Teachers are responsible for maintaining on-going records of attainment for the pupils in their own class. These should be locked away each night.

5. Resources

5.1. List of resources
A comprehensive list of equipment (with serial numbers if appropriate); books in stock; books in the library to support learning in this area: software, posters, videos, working models etc. available for teachers to use.

At Falmer Street County Primary we have managed to obtain at least one computer in each classroom, a concept keyboard in each class at Key Stage 1. We also have a ROAMER and three Pixies, a set of calculators and a set of documented software held centrally.

Central resources for exploiting the National Grid for Learning and information and communications technology are the responsibility of the IT coordinator. A small budget is made available each year and other coordinators are required to support ICT within their own subjects.

The school has additional concept keyboards for the use of Key Stage 1 classes, a video recorder, cameras and tape recorders along with master copies of all software in use

Health and safety issues in information technology include taking care with setting up and moving equipment, establishing appropriate working conditions and general electrical safety.

throughout the school. A library of software likely to be used infrequently by any one class, kits of hardware and associated software for control and measurement activities are available.

Children are not allowed to wheel computer trollies from one classroom to another.

No child may plug in or unplug electrical equipment.

5.2. Deployment of resources

Policy for who gets to use what, when and how, where they are stored, any security issues and map of distribution of software and hardware throughout the school may be included here.

Current computer hardware in school to be listed.

Teachers have agreed to swap systems if needed for particular purposes. In the library area there is a PC with a BT facility for video conferencing which was provided as part of a pilot scheme in which we were involved. Software is on order for this machine.

Computer trollies are bolted to the floor. The key is available from the office and they may be moved by teachers during the day but must be re-locked every evening.

Teachers will need to remove the computers from the store room each morning and relace them over night and at the weekend.

Teachers are insured to take home computers at any time providing they are not left overnight in a car or otherwise outside their place of residence.

5.3. Future purchasing policy

The school development plan sets out an objective of complete renewal of the computers in school over eight years.

We are committed to replace all BBC computers with A4000s by September 1998.

IT will be a priority area in 1998–99 and at that time . . .

A small fund is kept by the coordinator to extend or replace software as needs arise.

5.4.
Repair arrangements for equipment (with telephone numbers and necessary forms). Arrangements for safety checks on all electrical equipment.

We have an expensive contract for the repair of all of our computers. This is because we want to minimise the time that children may be without this facility. Teachers need to play their part in swiftly reporting any malfunction to the office who will arrange the repairs on their behalf.

Our contract allows for an annual safety check and unlimited repair services on all but our BBC machines. Please contact them yourself whenever you need their help.

5.5.
List of television and radio broadcasts (if appropriate).

Please inform the coordinator if the machine for which you are responsible malfunctions. She will endeavour to visit your area within the day.

6. Staff development

The successful implementation of the policy will probably need INSET, both school-based and using outside agencies. The policy document will appear more complete and credible if such arrangements are included here.

6.1.
A list of recommended books for teachers' personal reading.

Some suggestions can be found in Part 5.

Staff are encouraged to take computers home in order to prepare resources and develop personal competence and confidence in the use of IT.

An annual survey of staff INSET needs is undertaken by the coordinator and submitted to the school's professional development committee.

6.2.
The job description or agreed targets for the curriculum coordinator might be published here.

The coordinator will be available to discuss the use of any software between 3.30 and 4.00 pm each Thursday in her room.

Targets for INSET may be a feature of your school and expressed here as a spur to achievement.

6.3.
Name and addresses of support agencies which may offer advice or materials for teaching in your subject area.

The IT coordinator will be responsible for the implementation of the schools' ICT policy.

The coordinator will report to the governors on the progress of the implementation of the policy annually.

7. Review/evaluation of this policy

The headteacher and staff will need to review this policy to take account of changing circumstances. The date for its reconsideration may be stated here.

You might consider discussing with staff the inclusion of measures by which the success of the policy and its implementation may be judged. These may include teachers' and children's perceptions; children's work and other written evidence; a review of teachers' forecasts, parents' and governors' responses or classroom observation.

8. Declaration of policy

Wellford and Whickham Primary School's IT policy has been posted on the Internet. http://www.rmplc.co.uk/sites/wickham/policies/itpolicy.html.

There's a declaration of intent!

Part four

Monitoring and evaluation

Chapter 10 OFSTED re-inspection and the IT coordinator

> *Where teaching involving the use of IT is good, progression, pace, challenge, clarity of aim, differentiation and full participation are all features of the IT agenda . . . the use of IT is suitable and enhances learning. . . . and features regular monitoring and sensitive intervention.*
>
> (NAACE and NCET *Inspecting IT*, 1992)

In Part 1 we examined ways in which coordinators could audit the quality of current teaching and learning with and about IT in their own schools. Now we turn to external evaluation particularly that undertaken by OFSTED. By understanding the processes involved coordinators will improve their own ability to examine the state of their subjects and will be better prepared for the visit.

Although by now, all primary schools will have experienced their first OFSTED inspection, many individual teachers new to the profession, which includes a good proportion of IT coordinators, will not. This chapter is intended to assist those of you preparing for such an inspection and to give you and your staff an indication of the increased expectations implicit in subsequent rounds of the inspection process.

Throughout this chapter there are examples taken from inspection reports on a number of nursery, infant and primary schools with a range of provision for ICT.

Inspection Report

Attainment is well below national expectations at the end of both key stages and pupils do not experience the full range of activities in information technology. Reception and Key Stage 1 pupils do successfully use computers when given the opportunity and make appropriate responses to questions posed in games such as shape-matching programs designed to develop their logic and thinking skills. Key Stage 2 pupils use word processing, but the full potential of this application is not explored especially as much of the work consists of typing up previously written and corrected work. Pupils are still not competent at storing and retrieving information and rearranging text for presentation to a variety of audiences. There is no evidence of control, the use of spreadsheets, data handling in various contexts or the use of graphics to illustrate text and allow children to make the presentation of their written work more interesting. Overall, insufficient use is made of computers, many remaining unused for much of the school day. By the end of Year 6, pupils have made insufficient progress in the use of information technology.

Two-form entry primary and nursery school, June 1997: example of an inspection report on IT.

Section 9 (now 10) of the Education (Schools) Act 1992 requires all maintained primary schools to be inspected by Her Majesty's Chief Inspector (HMCI), working from the Office for Standards in Education (OFSTED). The act specifies that over a four year cycle (now increased to six years) schools will be inspected in order to identify their strengths and weaknesses, so helping them to improve the quality of the education they provide for pupils and thereby raise the standards achieved.

The inspection of IT in your school will examine the achievements and progress made by children in both key stages, their attitudes, the quality of the teaching they receive, the management and leadership provided, the accommodation and resources both hardware and software, and the effectiveness of the use made of those resources, alongside issues of equal opportunities and special educational needs. Not all of the judgments made about each of these features will appear in the report but they will be submitted to OFSTED in the subject profile, which is the evidence base for the report.

Clearly the IT coordinator is regarded by the OFSTED Framework as a key person within an overall responsibility for coordinating, monitoring and evaluating the school's provision. Inspectors will make judgments about

- the extent to which your leadership provides clear educational direction for the information technology work of the school;
- the way teaching and curriculum developments in ICT are monitored, evaluated and supported;
- the way in which the school's overall aims, values and policies are reflected through work promoted through the use of computers;
- the way the school, through its development planning, identifies relevant priorities and targets, takes the necessary action to implement them and monitors its progress towards them;
- whether there is a positive ethos, which reflects the school's commitment to high achievement, an effective learning environment, good relationships and equality of opportunity for all pupils, and
- whether all statutory requirements are met.

Inspection Report

The youngest pupils are able to operate a variety of programmes, use the mouse skilfully and by the time they have reached the end of Key Stage 1 they have developed ideas about the uses of computers in the world. At Key Stage 2, pupils have a good range of competence in word processing and computer operation. By the end of the key stage many pupils are more than able to find out information by the use of CD ROMs and can use the full range of facilities on most programmes to which they have been introduced.

Inspection report on IT.

Inspection Report

Information technology is used throughout the school to support learning in other curriculum areas. The standards attained by pupils in both key stages, and the progress achieved during their time in school, is in line with national expectations. Computers are used regularly in all classes. Most pupils are confident when using learning programmes on the computer. The youngest pupils work with equipment that allows them to create simple sentences. As they get older they develop satisfactory keyboard skills and manipulate the mouse control effectively. Pupils learn to load programmes from discs and can save and print their work. Word processing packages are employed to redraft writing. The older pupils use databases and produce graphs to illustrate their research findings. Small pocket book computers are used effectively by the older pupils to produce work for class projects.

Two-form entry primary school, June 1996.

The Framework for Inspection emphasises that a test of effective leadership and management is a commitment to monitoring and evaluating teaching and the curriculum and taking action to sustain and improve their quality. We may summarise these aspects of leadership as coordinating, monitoring and evaluating.

Coordinating

- developing an agreed view of what constitutes the school's ICT curriculum and its relationship to the National Curriculum;
- identifying principles and procedures for interrelating the constituent parts of the curriculum in relation to the pupils' opportunity to develop ICT capability;
- setting out principles and procedures for making and implementing curriculum decisions involving ICT between and within classes;
- establishing the roles and responsibilities of all those involved in curriculum decision making involving ICT;
- organising the IT curriculum to help achieve the aims of the school; provide coverage of the statutory curriculum; and, promote the educational achievement of pupils.

Monitoring

- monitoring teacher's planning and preparation to ensure that there is appropriate coverage of the IT and Programmes of Study of the statutory curriculum and appropriate balance between different aspects of work in IT;
- monitoring the work undertaken in classes to see how the work which has been planned and prepared is actually carried out and pupils' achievements assessed.

Evaluating

- evaluating the whole IT curriculum using the criteria of breadth, balance, continuity, progression, coherence and compliance with National Curriculum requirements;
- evaluation of the teaching techniques and organisational strategies employed by teachers, using the criterion of fitness for purpose;
- evaluating the standards and progress achieved in IT by individuals and groups and looking for trends and patterns of achievement;

- evaluating the overall quality of ICT provided including any extra curricula activity.
- evaluating the standards of IT across the school as a whole.

(adapted from Gadsby and Harrison, 1998)

The Framework is clear that it is the headteacher who is the educational leader responsible for the direction of the school's work and for its day to day management and organisation. In an effective school the headteacher has a direct concern for children's achievements and the sustained improvement in the quality of teaching and learning in all areas of the curriculum including IT. Thus many of the above expectations will be **about the system of which you are a part rather than you personally**. However, all staff such as coordinators will have delegated leadership and management functions which form part of the above set of responsibilities and therefore it is important to know, just as outlined in Part 1 of this book, those for which you are responsible and those in which you play a part alongside others (classteachers and senior managers for example).

What can an IT coordinator do to make sure that ICT appears in the best possible light and that if there are weaknesses the inspector charged with the responsibility for leading the team in their examination of ICT, fully understands that you are on top of them?

Firstly, IT coordinators should try to make the time to look at their subject areas in the same way that OFSTED inspectors will. This is laid out in the Subject Profile that has to be completed by inspectors looking at the core subject but in practice is a record of inspection evidence collected for all the National Curriculum subjects.

The subject profile

Inspectors are required to construct a subject profile which summarises evidence and declares judgments about set criteria for each of the core subjects and it is common practice for contractors to require this record of evidence for each of the other subjects inspected. The subject profile consists of the following sections (see Figure 10.1):

The Subject Profile

Attainment and progress:
evidence of attainment in relation to national standards or expectations; evidence of pupils' progress in relation to prior attainment.

Attitudes, behaviour and personal development:
evidence of pupils' attitudes to learning in the subject, behaviour, quality of relationships and other aspects of personal development;

Teaching:
evidence of the strengths and weaknesses in the teaching of the subject;

The curriculum and assessment:
evidence of strengths and weaknesses of curriculum planning in the subject, and of procedures for and accuracy of assessing pupils' progress in the subject.

Pupils' spiritual, moral, social and cultural development:
summary of evidence and findings of the subject's contribution to the provision for pupils' spiritual, moral, social and cultural development.

Leadership and management:
evidence of how well leadership, management and coordination of the subject contribute to the quality of the provision and then educational standards achieved.

Staffing, accommodation and learning resources:
evidence of the quality of staffing, accommodation and resources and the effects of any good or poor provision on the quality of education and the educational standards achieved in the subject.

Efficiency:
summary of evidence and findings as to how efficiently and effectively the resources made available for the subject are managed and deployed.

FIG 10.1
Monitoring the quality of ICT

- Attainment and progress
- Attitudes, behaviour and personal development
- Teaching
- The curriculum and assessment
- Pupil's spiritual, moral, social and cultural development
- Leadership and management
- Staffing accommodation and resources
- Efficiency

The profile is expanded below.

Inspection Report

Standards are in line with national expectations at Key Stage 1 and rise above expectations at Key Stage 2. Pupils achieve appropriate levels for their abilities at Key Stage 1 whilst many achieve higher than expected for their ability at Key Stage 2.

One-form entry church school, March 1996.

Attainment and progress

Inspectors will seek evidence of the children's **attainment** in IT in relation to National Expectations. Can the children use equipment and software competently and confidently to perform a range of tasks? Do children in discussion — show awareness of the ways ICT can be used in the world of work? Are substantial proportions of pupils in Y2 and Y6 able to demonstrate the levels of competence set out in the level descriptors for Levels 2 and 4 respectively? Is the degree of variation between pupils acceptable — has any variation to do with gender, ethnicity, age, classes to which they have assigned, access to equipment?

Can you identify aspects within strands of IT where children are achieving at Level 5? Are there some above these levels, what proportion are below? How can you show that they have reached these levels of competence? What records, wall displays, computer files of children's work have you got to show?

Advice on judging standards in IT is available to both inspectors and coordinators the SCAA booklet *Expectations in IT at Key Stages 1 and 2*. Elements of this publication are used in the next chapter. However, when teachers have made those judgments about what individual children know and can do what becomes of the records? Do you routinely look to see how children's achievements increase as they pass through the school? Do you have an overview of standards? Do you know how much progress children make between say Y4 and Y6? Is this *all* children, largely the boys or mostly children with access to computers at home?

Evidence of pupils' **progress** may be considered in a number of ways:

- In lessons — where specific points have been taught do children show learning gains?
- Over a year — as evidenced in books, files, and displays — are children clearly more capable than they were before?
- Across the key stage — do children develop a range of skills, knowledge and understanding as they move through the classes?

Inspection Report

The pupils respond positively when given the opportunity to work with technology. They are confident, eager and work well as individuals, pairs or small groups. They are proud of what they produce and maintain a high-level of concentration when engaged in productive tasks. They handle equipment with care. Those children with special educational needs receive effective support in class from classroom and special needs assistants.

Information technology is being developed to extend learning through a carefully structured and practical plan. There is a draft policy statement and scheme of work. This matches the requirements of the National Curriculum. The co-ordinator has only recently taken over responsibility for the subject. Areas for development have been identified and include training and the purchase of additional resources when funds are available.

Two-form entry primary, June 1996.

Can you show that children make significant learning gains in any of these time frames? Can you demonstrate that children are making sufficient progress to ensure that national expectations will be met at the end of their key stages.

Evidence of **progress in relation to prior attainment** will be sought in order to see whether pupils with special educational needs for example, are being given the opportunity to demonstrate IT capability and those children who have found IT work difficult in the past are able to make appropriate progress, sometimes through differentiated work or additional support. Some pupils who are particularly advanced in their work can be seen to continue to make additional progress when they are supported in their need to access more advanced skills and techniques.

Attitudes, behaviour and personal development

Here inspectors will be seeking evidence of pupils' attitudes to learning when using computer and other ICT equipment. What is evident about the quality of the relationships between children when working together on ICT projects? What other personal development is related to the way ICT is used and exploited? When considering attitudes inspectors will observe the ways students approach their tasks. Do they demonstrate commitment to achievement, persevere and cooperate with others? Do children, through the use of ICT, pose questions, attempt to solve problems and work collaboratively? Is concentration short-lived and the computer viewed as a toy rather than a tool? Can pupils articulate choices to use or not to use the computer to achieve certain ends? Do they use the opportunity which ICT affords for trial and experimentation systematically to improve their work or in a random fashion? Are children active participants in lessons, can they evaluate their own work according to their age and do they demonstrate a measure of responsibility for their own learning?

Teaching

Evidence of strengths and weaknesses in the teaching of IT throughout the school will be sought through direct observation and discussion and scrutiny of teachers' planning

Inspection Report

Displays around the school do not foster computer literacy, children do not routinely experience worksheets generated by use of the computer or other computer output and there are few books in the school library about IT and its applications in everyday life. Many of the children have access to computers at home but this is not exploited so they do not bring their skills, knowledge and experience into the educational context in order to further their own development and that of their peers in the classroom. This is a wasted opportunity.

Two-form entry JMI and N, June 1997.

and records and examples of children's work in ICT. IT coordinators who would like to 'inspect' their own schools might wish to consider the following dimensions of teaching:

Planning

How does each teacher decide what learning is appropriate at what times for which pupils? How does the work seen at the time of your observation relate to previous work, work in parallel classes, work in the rest of the school by older/younger pupils? Does planning take account of the National Curriculum; prior attainment by pupils; the work being undertaken by the rest of the class; and, or, the school's scheme of work? Are children given the opportunity to use familiar techniques in unfamiliar contexts? Is computer use considered merely as a reward or just a means of occupying pupils?

Aims

Do the learning aims suggest certain activities or are the tasks driven by a limited range of available activities? Are the expected learning outcomes appropriate for the age and abilities of the children? What previous knowledge, understanding, skills will children need to have in order to complete the tasks? Are the tasks differentiated to challenge different pupils?

Assessment opportunities

Are opportunities created to determine the extent of the learning gained by individual pupils? How is this recorded? Are teachers able to differentiate between attainment in IT and attainment in the subject area used as the current context and supported by ICT? Are assessments used to inform subsequent planning?

Pace

What rate of learning is evident? Do teachers press children by sensitive intervention and appropriate challenge to quickly move on to new skills and uses of ICT? Are all opportunities used to allow children to develop their capability? Do children spend considerable time repeating familiar work or techniques? Are children given the chance to progress by being encouraged to suggest alternatives and extensions to their own work?

Inspection Report

IT has been given a high priority in the school's development plan, although this development is not costed, and it is proposed that an LEA policy document be introduced to staff in the new academic year. This will be insufficient in itself to raise the level of pupils' capability. Nothing less than a whole school approach which commits every teacher to play their part in a continuous systematic process, building up children's skills and developing their competencies is needed. Every subject in the National Curriculum provides opportunities for pupils to develop and apply their IT capability. Children are entitled to use these opportunities. Curriculum coordinators in each subject will need to ensure that their own subject plays its part.

Two-form entry primary with nursery, June 1997.

Homework

What use is made of the fact that many children will have access to computers and other IT equipment at home? Do teachers use this wider knowledge of the use of ICT as a means to help the whole class to understand the role of computers in society and specific uses to which technology can be put? Are children set tasks which involve research at home?

Teachers' own knowledge

Are all teachers capable and confident in their own use of ICT? Do they all understand the part they individually play in promoting children's development as they pass through the school? Can teachers use computers to create their own worksheets, label displays, write reports? Are they all aware of the school's planned scheme of work?

Organisation for learning

How is access to computers and other ICT peripherals organised? What ways do children have to know when it is their turn, how are records kept, are all available times used to maximise access? Do all pupils have the chance to take the lead in passing on knowledge of new applications to their peers? How does the work of the rest of the class relate to the work going on at the computer? Are pupils being asked to perform irrelevant or mundane tasks in order to notch up time in ICT rather than to contribute to the current work of the class?

By considering these dimensions IT coordinators may be able to gain an insight into the way the quality of teaching will be perceived by visiting inspectors.

The curriculum and assessment

In this section inspectors are required to declare their judgments on the strengths and weaknesses in the IT curriculum and its planning and the procedures for and accuracy of, the assessment of pupils' progress.

Judgments about the quality and range of the curriculum are crucial to you in your role as coordinator. Your knowledge and understanding of what goes on where, what follows from which aspects of capability will be sought by the inspector.

Inspection Report

There is no current policy or scheme of work to support systematic teaching of information technology skills. There are no formal arrangements within classes to ensure all children experience the few programmes which are used and no proper assessment of pupils' progress is undertaken. The curriculum does not meet statutory requirements in that it does not address all strands of the National Curriculum.

Two-form entry primary with nursery, June 1997.

Here are some questions which I, in my role as inspector, would be likely to ask, and to which you should know the answers:

What exactly is the difference between the aspects of word processing being taught in Y3 and in Y6? Are children achieving these skills and are you satisfied with this rate of progress?

When in your school are children taught to use LOGO and where in the school are these skills built upon? What remedial action is taken for those who fall behind? How do skills learned here relate to Programmes of Study in other curricular areas?

How do you know whether the desired competences to be reached by the end of Y1/4/6 have been taught? What do you do with this information?

Which aspects of graphical communication are used in Key Stage 1 and which in Key Stage 2? Where is the evidence to be found?

What programs are usually employed to help children to develop a capability in data handling and how does this relate to the mathematics curriculum?

How are records of children's achievements in ICT used by the next class teacher in planning individual pupil's work? Does this system work? How does each subject coordinator ensure that work in his/her subject contributes to pupils' ICT capability development and how does the use of ICT relate to support for each subject? What meetings are held to ensure this takes place? (see Figure 10.2)

How frequently do pupils use the computers available? How does this add up over the period of a year?

One of the ways in which IT coordinators have found it useful (some along with their staffs) to consider the quality of their curriculum provision is through the negative. That is: what would you consider to be an unsatisfactory curriculum? NAACE and NCET's booklet *Inspecting IT* gives us a start:

An unsatisfactory curriculum exists where all pupils are not given opportunities to acquire IT capability appropriate to their needs and abilities. The curriculum is also unsatisfactory where

FIG 10.2
Evidence of IT in the classroom

Things to look for in the classroom

Is the computer, trolley, printer etc. mounted, positioned safely?

Is there suitable seating at the computer?

Does the computer have a home in the room?
Posters? Helpful notices? Books about computers? Disc boxes?

Is the printer quiet? fast? good quality?

Are there examples of computer work on the walls?

Is there any evidence that the teacher makes personal or professional use of computers?

Do the children talk freely about the computer?

Do the children attempt to solve problems on the computer? Do they rely on the teacher?

Can the children use the mouse?

Can they find their way around software, menus etc?

Can the children use the printer?

Can the children save files?

Is there evidence of text handling? data handling? other strands?

Does the teacher teach at the computer?

Is there evidence that these children have progressed in IT?

Are any peripherals in evidence?

achievement with IT is limited by the range and degree of challenge offered to pupils. Poor continuity occurs where pupils are taught to use software without reference to their previous experience, where too much time elapses before skills are consolidated, or where gaps in provision occur. Limited opportunities occur when a wide variety of subject contexts is not exploited to develop IT capacity

Look through the extracts of real OFSTED reports in boxes in the left-hand column in this chapter. What other unsatisfactory aspects can you list? Do any apply to your school?

Pupils' spiritual, moral, social and cultural development

Inspectors will seek to determine the ways in which work in ICT contributes to the school's provision for pupils' spiritual, moral, social and cultural development.

Inspection Report

Children are not currently receiving their entitlement in information technology. The school has sufficient computers for one machine per classroom but these are not used enough to allow children to develop capability in this area. The range of software owned by the school is not sufficient to allow the full use of IT applications to support all areas of the curriculum. There is little opportunity for children to develop their skills in word processing, store and access their work for future editing, use LOGO or other work to develop capability in control applications. The school currently does not meet the National Curriculum requirements in this area.

One-form entry primary, February 1997.

As discussed in Chapter 4, used creatively ICT can enhance primary pupils' repertoire of learning skills; increase access to the curriculum for children with a variety of individual needs and from diverse cultural heritages. In primary schools its effective use can force teachers to confront many of the challenges of today. It has, for example been argued elsewhere that group work can help schools to value cultural diversity explicitly and to encourage children to value themselves as part of human kind, which celebrates both similarities and differences. Group work around a computer can help to encourage children to look for strategies for resolving problems, especially conflicts and to capitalise on cooperative communalities. Using the Internet or CD ROM encyclopaedias can help children to discover aspects of their own culture, particularly those which help them to locate themselves and, used sensitively, to foster empathy by imagining the feelings of people both in similar and different situations to their own. Thus there are ways in which IT coordinators can promote these aspects of school provision.

Leadership and management

The opening sections of this chapter set out quite clearly the way in which the OFSTED framework requires inspectors to look at management and leadership within the subject and IT coordinators will be well advised to discuss their roles further with the headteacher to ensure that there is no misunderstanding and that time, if required for successful completion of the tasks, is allocated in advance. ACITT's amplification of good and poor management in the subject appeared in Chapter 3, but inspectors will be likely to look further, for example:

- how does the school's ICT policy fit in with the other documents available; does it reflect the school's values?
- is there consistency amongst staff as to the way ICT is approached?
- are all teachers clear about their individual contribution to pupils' development?
- are there structures to determine if teachers need help and what support is provided for them?
- what time do you have to carry out your role?

Inspection Report

The school benefits from an enthusiastic cocoordinator, who, with the support of the senior management team has been able to enhance the confidence of other members of staff. The agreed policy statement and scheme of work developed by the cocoordinator strongly guides the work of teachers, ensuring both continuity and progression.

One-form entry CE Primary, 1996.

- what financial structures are in place to ensure that the school can benefit from emerging technology?
- how is the current hardware managed; what repair systems are in place; how are decisions about new software made?

Staffing accommodation and resources

In this part of the subject profile inspectors are required to summarise evidence and state judgments about the quantity and quality of staffing (both teaching and non-teaching), accommodation and resources. The effects on standards of any good or poor provision are critical features of this section.

It is usual for inspectors to be given a list of the qualifications of teachers and to enquire about additional courses undertaken especially by the National Curriculum subject coordinators. Judgments will be made about the degree of competence of teachers to use ICT in support of their teaching. Differences between the curriculum provided for different pupils because of their particular teacher's preferences or lack of training are not acceptable. The key questions for you to consider are:

- what are teachers' current competences in ICT?
- what are they expected to teach?
- what support can you provide to help them to teach it effectively?

Unsatisfactory provision and poor use of support staff may result in teachers' own time being used ineffectively, whereas the use of trained adult helpers has been shown to be effective in a number of situations.

As well as the courses attended by you, inspectors will examine the list of courses and Inset activity by your colleagues. Have you been able to arrange specific training for them — what has the effect of this been on the curriculum and children's achievements?

Accommodation issues include access and suitability of siting of sockets in classrooms. It may also involve a discussion on the housing, storage and timetabling of scarce resources such as colour printers and input devices. Lighting should be considered and ventilation will need to be adequate to ensure that computers do not cause an undue rise in air temperature in the summer.

Inspection Report

The provision of computers and ancillary equipment is adequate, although as a more coherent approach to teaching and learning with and about computers is adopted the need will become apparent for higher quality printers and greater access to machines capable of using CD ROMs for research and reference. The quality, quantity and range of software owned by the school is poor. In many subject areas there are no suitable programs and what there are is not always known to teachers and thus does not feature in their teaching plans. Lack of software means pupils have no experience in the use of clip-art or simulation programmes in other curricular areas.

Two-form entry JMI and N, June 1997.

At present the school is not making full use of the investment in hardware and thus the financial cost is not justified. As pupils make little progress from reception to Y6 and yet IT is one of the most expensive subjects to resource, the school gives poor value for money in this respect.

Two-form entry primary with nursery, June 1997.

Statistical data given to inspectors by OFSTED will reveal the level of hardware in your school and compare it (pupil to computer ratio) to that in other schools both locally and nationally. Of course this crude statistic will not reveal the range of machines, the peripherals and the accompanying software and your inspector will be particularly keen to discuss with you the match between curriculum needs and the provision.

The IT policy should indicate how the school makes sure that all staff are aware of the range of equipment available. Inspectors will want to verify that the management (location, access, security and supervision) of ICT equipment promotes its efficient use. Health and safety considerations are pertinent here. Equipment should be checked regularly.

Software copyright is a major issue for schools. All members of staff should be aware of their responsibilities with respect to copyright (see Chapter 7).

Efficiency

This is the summary of evidence and findings as to how efficiently and effectively the ICT resources are managed and deployed.

How frequently are computers used? What ways do children have to know when it is their turn, how are records kept, are all available times used to maximise access? Is the software well used to teach certain concepts or skills?

How are judgments made within the school to see whether finances made available to support ICT teaching and learning are used in the most effective way? What do you or the senior managers in your school do to determine whether the money for IT has been effective in promoting children's learning? Are future purchases based upon such information?

In addition inspectors have to complete a subject summary form rating from 1 (excellent) to 7 (poor) each of the following aspects. What is your score for each of these? (Figure 10.3)

Grade 1	Excellent			
Grade 2	Very good	Favourable	Well above average	Promotes very high standards and quality
Grade 3	Good			
Grade 4	Satisfactory	Broadly Typical	Average	Promotes sound standards and quality
Grade 5	Unsatisfactory			
Grade 6	Poor	Unfavourable	Well below average	Promotes low standards and quality
Grade 7	Very poor			

	KS1	KS2	Overall
EDUCATIONAL STANDARDS ACHIEVED			
Attainment			
Progress			
Progress of pupils with SEN			
Attitude, behaviour and personal development			
QUALITY of EDUCATION			
Teaching			
The curriculum			
Assessment			
MANAGEMENT and EFFICIENCY			
Leadership and management			
Staffing accommodation and learning resources			
Efficiency			

Components of teaching	KS1	KS2
Teachers' knowledge and understanding		
Teachers' expectations		
Teachers' planning		
Methods and organisation of teaching		
Management of pupils		
Use of time and resources		
Quality and use of day to day assessment		
Use of homework		

Components of judgments about the IT curriculum	KS1	KS2
Breadth and balance of IT curriculum		
Equality of access and opportunity		
Components of judgments about the IT curriculum		
Provision for pupils with SEN		
Planning for progression and continuity		

Components of judgments about assessment	KS1	KS2
Procedures for assessing pupil's attainment		
Use of assessments to inform curriculum planning		

	Overall
Contribution of IT to pupils' SMSC Development	

Components of judgments about leadership and management	Overall
Leadership: clear educational direction for IT in the school	
Support and monitoring of teaching and curriculum development in IT	
Development planning, monitoring and evaluation	
The ethos for learning	

Components of staffing, accommodation and learning resources	Overall
Match of number, qualifications and experience of teachers to the demands of the IT curriculum	
Components of staffing, accommodation and learning resources	
Match of number, qualifications and experience of support staff to the demands of the IT curriculum	
Arrangements for the professional development of staff	
Adequacy of accommodation for the effective teaching of IT	
Adequacy of resources for effective teaching of IT	
Components of efficiency	
Use of teaching and support staff	
Use of learning resources and accommodation	

Is there recorded evidence of significant variations in any of the following?	Yes or No
Attainment or progress of girls and boys?	
Attainment or progress of different ethnic groups?	
Overall attainment over time?	
Progress of pupils of differing attainment?	
Is there non-compliance with the National Curriculum?	
Is there non-compliance with Health and Safety requirements?	

FIG 10.3
Proforma for judging efficiency of IT provision

(reproduced by kind permission of OFSTED)

Chapter 11 Preparing for an OFSTED re-inspection

In the previous chapter IT coordinators were encouraged to adopt many of the methods of inspectors when considering their school's ICT provision. This chapter will help them to prepare when re-inspected so that they can present their achievements in the best possible light.

Before the inspection

You will have between six years (if your school has recently been inspected) and two terms to prepare for your next inspection. Needless to say, the most effective preparation for any inspection is to do your job as well as you can over a period of time (Gadsby and Harrison, 1998). Eventually however, a registered inspector will contact your school to negotiate a date and sooner or later you will be told the size of the team and how many days the inspection will last. A typical urban primary school might have four or five inspectors over four to five days. One of the inspectors will be a 'lay' inspector, i.e. a person who has had no professional association with schools. Lay inspectors tend to spend less time in the school and frequently do not have responsibility for a curriculum area, however they are full inspectors and will have an equal say in the formation of the corporate judgments upon which the report will be founded. Thus the team will be continually sharing evidence and the judgments they make before, during and after the inspection week. In terms of cross-curricular ICT, this is most appropriate. Indeed many teams keep a list of the ways in which ICT has been seen to be used in classrooms whatever the main focus of their observation.

A typical deployment may look like this:

Registered Inspector:	Science; PE; Attainment & progress; Leadership and Management; Teaching;
Team member 1:	Mathematics; IT; D & T; geography; efficiency; staffing, accommodation and resources; attitudes and personal development,
Team member 2:	English, music, art, history; curriculum and assessment, areas of learning for the under fives;
Lay Inspector:	Pupil's spiritual, moral, social and cultural development; support guidance and pupils' welfare; attendance; partnership with parents and the community.

Readers will see that while the second inspector will be responsible for completion of the IT subject summary and write the paragraph on IT, the evidence contained within it will need to be in agreement with the findings of the other inspectors who, while looking at other subjects and aspects, will contribute to the evidence base about IT. Likewise, inspector 2's evidence about leadership, the curriculum etc. in IT will combine with findings in other subject areas to the corporate judgments about such matters across the school as a whole. Thus you can expect inspectors to collaborate and cooperate closely together — getting ready to put on a show for one week and for one inspector is not likely to be effective preparation.

When the dates for the inspection have been arranged the RgI will make his or her initial visit to the school, which will usually involve a tour of the classrooms to meet with the staff. Although not officially part of the inspection, who can dismiss completely their first impressions? When you know this visit is about to take place you should make sure that the RgI is given the chance to observe what you want him or her to see! Largely this initial meeting is taken up with talking to the head teacher. The agenda I use is reproduced below:

Agenda for Inspectors initial meeting

Introductions

The inspection team, experience and contractor introductions.

- The school, staff, governors, issues and recent developments
- Characteristics of the school, transfers in and out
- SEN IEPs
- Buildings, priorities, times of the school day, school roll etc.

Procedures and methods of inspection

- before the inspection week —
  HT form, HT statement, curriculum documents, plans (layout), teachers' timetables, school visits/extra-curricular etc. teachers' records, reports etc., preparation of children's books A, AA, AAA
- during the week
  - observations in classrooms
  - interviews with staff and governors
  - review of children's work and discussions with children
  - teachers' planning and record keeping
- after the inspection
  - feedback to HT, SMT, governors
  - publishing the report
  - action plan

Agree future dates and arrangements for meetings/parents' questionnaire

staff, and governors' meeting
parents' meeting
inspection team meeting

Domestic arrangements

room, lunches, services, payments

Currently available documents/brochure/staff lists?

Headteacher's issues

Later meetings will be arranged to speak with the teaching staff, the governors and a further meeting with the headteacher is often arranged to clarify any outstanding issues especially those thrown up by the statistical information provided by OFSTED to both the RgI and the school. The date for a meeting with parents will be set and arrangements made for a questionnaire to be distributed to parents. The questions are in standard form.

	Parents' questionnaires					
		strongly agree	agree	neither	disagree	strongly disagree
1	I feel that the school encourages parents to play an active part in the life of the school					
2	I would find it easy to approach the school with problems or questions to do with my child(ren)					
3	The school handles complaints from parents well					
4	The school gives me a clear understanding of what is taught					
5	The school keeps me well informed about my child(ren)'s progress					
6	The school enables my children to achieve a good standard of work					
7	The school encourages children to get involved in more than just their daily lessons					
8	I am satisfied with the work my child(ren) is/are expected to do at home					
9	The school's values have a positive effect on my child(ren)					
10	The school achieves a high standard of good behaviour					
11	My child(ren) like(s) school					

(reproduced with permission of OFSTED)

The following list of documents will be asked for:

- a statement from the headteacher and details as required on the head's form;
- the school's prospectus;
- school development plan;
- a copy of the governors' last annual report to parents;
- minutes of the governors' meetings for the past twelve months;
- staff handbook;
- curriculum plans, policies and guidelines or schemes of work, already in existence;
- other policy documents which are available in the school;

Inspection Report

Standards of attainment are below national expectations in both key stages. By the end of Key Stage 1 pupils can talk about some uses of computers in everyday life and are able to operate the mouse and make selections from on-screen menus. They can also make appropriate responses to questions posed in adventure games and shape-matching programs by using the keyboard but too many are unable to work confidently with text processors, create pictures or print out the results of their work. By the end of Key Stage 2 pupils are able to interrogate a CD ROM encyclopaedia and although some work is undertaken with upper juniors in databases and information handling their lack of earlier work in this area means that their achievements are not at a level of IT capability as set out in the National Curriculum for children of their age.

Nevertheless pupils respond well to IT. They enjoy using computers, talk enthusiastically about its applications and are able to work cooperatively in pairs when given the opportunity. However teaching both with and about IT is unsatisfactory. Teachers are not confident in their own use of IT for creating worksheets and labelling displays and do not readily adopt computers for the teaching of other subjects. Therefore computers are used too infrequently, many opportunities to use computers are missed and once pupils are working on the computer they seldom receive the help they need in order to make progress.

Two-form entry CE Primary, 1997.

- a programme or timetable of the work of the school for the period of the inspection (deadline to be negotiated);
- other information the school wishes to be considered, such as school self-evaluation activities.

You should check well in advance (now?) that what you want to be said about the use of computers in your school is suitably recorded. For example is ICT a priority in the current SDP; does it feature in the budget plan; do ICT related issues regularly appear on the agendas of staff meetings; do governors take an interest and are such discussions featured in minutes; are there references to ICT in the documents relating to other curriculum areas? Documents which are likely to have most relevance to your role will be curriculum plans, policies and guidelines and schemes of work. You may also wish to check your teaching and learning policy and those for assessment, equal opportunities, SEN, and multi-cultural education.
You are not restricted to the list of documents above, although *OFSTED* do restrict inspection teams from asking for more.
If there are other papers which help to explain the work you are doing to support teaching and learning with ICT make sure these are included.

Before the inspection the RgI will ask for the school and class timetables of teaching taking place in the week concerned to be made available and distributed to the inspection team. There is no need for schools to alter their normal work pattern but you will need to check these closely to determine just what ICT activities will be taking place during the inspection week. If nothing else you should know what is being taught and how it relates to the school plan and if by chance very little is going on then you will need to be able to explain this and have examples available to demonstrate that the children do indeed receive a full and balanced curriculum.

Finally the RgI will give the school, in advance of the inspection itself, a timetable for the discussions that will be likely to take place with individual members of staff and the arrangements for looking at children's work, current planning, pupils' records and reports, individual education plans and assessment documents.

The inspection week

When the team arrive in school they will almost certainly spend more than the required 60 per cent of time in direct observation of teaching and learning in classrooms. This will help them to confirm or deny their hypotheses formed on the basis of the pre-inspection evidence. As well as watching teachers teach they will discuss children's work with them in individual and group discussions; hear a sample of children read; scrutinise a sample of work from each year group; look at current plans and teacher's records; attend assemblies; watch the children at play and before and after school; sit with children at lunchtime; look at annual reports to parents; follow through individual education plans to see whether pupils are receiving the additional input and annual reviews they require; see whether teachers' plans match the reality; examine whether baseline assessments and National Curriculum test results are built upon in subsequent classes, and have individual discussions with staff especially those with management responsibilities.
This means you.

What sort of questions will you be asked? I have reproduced here a typical agenda I used recently. I give it to the coordinator the previous day so that they can look up any thing they might have forgotten.

Agenda for discussion between Ms X, Primary School Information Technology Coordinator and Mike Harrison inspector with responsibility for coordinating the report on Information Technology — Wednesday 08:15

1. Brief description of your background, qualifications, training and experience.
2. Brief description of your role in the school as Information Technology coordinator. Ongoing advice and support to colleagues; gathering information and research reports; providing teaching in ICT; modelling good teaching in the use of computers to support learning; evaluation of coverage/strands; developing assessment techniques; moderating work through the collection of samples; developing teaching approaches?

3 Who is responsible for the quality of teaching with computers throughout the school? Who is responsible for children's progress in Information Technology? Do you teach LOGO; use data bases/spreadsheets? Where is this recorded?
4 What is the effect of not having a policy or scheme of work for the use of ICT in the school? How do you know all staff are doing it? What planning processes are usual? How have the two new computer systems been utilised? What do you expect the result to be — on achievement; on progress; on teachers' levels of understanding?
5 How do you influence other teachers in the use of Information Technology? How do you ensure a continuous programme between classes, between KS1 and KS2 and progression of knowledge and skills? How do you get an overview of standards?
6 Do you have a role in monitoring teachers' plans, pupils' work? What actually happens? What use is made of Information Technology for children with special difficulties?
7 How are IT resources managed? Budget, audit; organisation; ordering; replenishment; distribution; emergencies?
8 What Information Technology Inset has been provided; how were ICT Inset needs identified? What has been provided in school; in other institutions; have you led any sessions?
9 Please comment on any links with the community; other schools; use of the environment?
10 What are your aims for development of the school's Information Technology curriculum? How will you know if you have achieved them? What needs doing next?
11 How do you record children's progress in Information Technology and report it to parents?

During the week each inspector is attempting to describe the standards achieved and the cause of those standards being as they are. The first priority is to assess and evaluate the school's outcomes i.e. what pupils achieve, in particular their attainment at the end of each key stage and the progress they are making. This provides the basis for considering why achievements are as they are, in particular, how effective teaching is, and how leadership and management impact on the quality of provision and what is achieved. Ofsted's *Improving the Efficiency and Effectiveness of Inspection* displays this diagrammatically. (Figure 11.1)

Educational standards achieved	Attitudes, behaviour and personal delopment		Attainment and progress	Attendance	
Provision	Curriculum and assessment	Spiritual, moral, social and cultural development	Teaching	Support guidance and pupil's welfare	Partnership with parents and community
Management	Staffing accommodation and resources		Leadership	Efficiency	

FIG 11.1
Assessing outcomes

Thus everything stems from what the children know, can do and understand. However, the inspectors will only be able to make the sort of judgments about pupil's attainment that you and the rest of your staff can. They do not have a magic wand. They will look at the work provided, the displays on the walls and talk with children engaged in ICT and attempt to determine how close they are to achieving the national expectations especially at Year 2 and Year 6.

SCAA has produced a booklet which illustrates those expectations exemplifying the level descriptions which form part of the National Curriculum. Some examples are given here (Figure 11.2):

	By the end of year 2	By the end of year 4	By the end of year 6
Key characteristic	Children can **work purposefully** and confidently with IT to achieve specific outcomes. Children investigate options and describe the effects of their actions and experiences of using IT.	Use IT to **develop ideas**. Children follow lines of enquiry, make **decisions** and take the results of those decisions into account in successive steps, and describe their use of IT.	Children can **interpret** the information obtained from an information system and question its plausibility, and **compare** use of IT with other methods.
Communicating information	Understand that information can be presented in different forms, and use IT to help them generate and communicate ideas in different forms, for example writing, creating pictures or sounds, presenting tables of results.	Use IT to generate, amend, organise and present ideas, for example producing a short piece of writing, laying out the text, checking for sense and spellings, correcting as necessary, or developing a poster design using a paint package.	Use IT to combine different forms of information, for example using graphic images to complement text or combining sound with pictures to create multimedia presentations. Show an awareness of audience, for example when choosing layout, typeface or graphics.

FIG 11.2
Level descriptions

The SCAA booklet similarly describes handling information, controlling and monitoring and modelling at the end of these years. Illustrations of children's work follow and are annotated with key elements for judgments to be made. Thus inspectors armed with such assistance will take their findings to the team and attempt to get the whole inspection team to agree on the final judgments about your subject. Inspection week will end with feedback to key individuals and at this stage you will be made familiar with the main findings and the key issues that will appear in the report.

When the report is published

If after the above process is over you can agree with Graham Dean (1996) that the inspection told us only what we know already, you will be well on the way to writing the action plan needed in response to the report. It will indeed be a replica of your school development plan and as such will cause you little additional work. If, however, some elements of your school's provision are found to be unsatisfactory you will wish to use this information to enhance your claim on the additional funds that will be at your school's disposal in the year following the inspection.

What you should do will depend upon the key issues identified. But you may start by re-reading some parts of this book!

Part five Resources for learning

Chapter 12
Useful addresses

Chapter 12 Useful addresses

Primary schools will have been buying computers over the past ten years under the influence of the Department of Trade and Industry which offered schools 50 per cent discounts on certain makes; LEAs who attempted to create homogenous provision of machines across all primary schools in the county in order to simplify software purchase, training and technical issues; and the individual preferences of headteachers and previous coordinators. The constraints of money, technical know-how and security issues will also have contributed to the particular pattern of provision you will find in your school. It is unlikely that you will be the sole decider about any possible future purchases but you will want to present an opinion to show that you are on top of the job you have been given.

You will be best advised to help whoever will take the final decision by setting out the important factors as you see them (see Figure 12.1).

You might list them as:

To think about	Make your case here
How does the new proposed machine fit into the current pattern of provision?	
Are any of the proposed purchases about to be technically superseded by superior machines and what this might imply;	
Is there educational software currently available for the proposed computers and will you need to purchase programmes specifically for new machines;	
Will additional training be necessary for staff to use any new type of machine and where such training can be purchased;	
How the prices compare across the model ranges. Are the extra facilities worth the additional cash over the lower-priced models?	

FIG 12.1
Deciding factors when considering IT purchases

There is no need, unless asked, to recommend one specific purchase — if you make an honest attempt to detail the relevant criteria and involve the teachers who would be most likely to have access to the new machine, you can leave the final decision to those who hold the reins of power and can argue the case for this or that particular computer with various staff.

An option you might like to put before the senior management team is to purchase a number of small hand-held 'palmtop computers' in preference to the larger desktop ones we are used to. The portability of these computers, the versatility of their in-built software and usage, along with the fact that they can be easily linked to larger machines for transfer of data make them a choice to be considered, especially if your school has already reached the stage of having one desktop machine per classroom. (Cross and Birch, 1994; NCET, 1994)

Some suppliers of hardware and peripherals are listed below:

Acer (UK) Maddison House Thomas Road HP10 0PE Tel.: 0168 533422	**Acorn Computers** C/o Exemplar Education The Quorum, Barnwell Road Cambridge CB5 8RE	**Apple Computers** 2 Furzeground Rd, Stockley Park, Uxbridge Middlesex UB11 1BE
Bandai (UK) Jellicoe House Botleigh Grange Hed End Southampton SO30 2AF	**Canon (UK) Ltd** The Harlequin Centre Southall Lane, Middlesex UB2 5NH	**Compaq** Hotham House Heron Square Richmond Surrey TW9 1EJ
Dawson's Music, 65 Sankey Street, Warrington, Cheshire WA1 1SU	**Deltronics,** Church Road Ind Estate, Gorlas, Llanelli, Dyfed, SA14 7NN	**Research Machines** Hitchin Court New Mill House 183 Milton Park Abingdon OX14 4SE
Swallow Systems 134 Cock Lane High Wycombe Buckinghamshire HP13 7EA Tel.: 01494 813471	**TAG Developments Ltd,** 25 Pelham Road, Gravesend, Kent, DA11 0HU Tel.: 01474 357350; 0800 591262	**Valiant Technology Ltd** Valiant House, 3 Grange Mills Weir Road London SW12 0NE

Software issues

Whereas the headteacher and/or governors may want you to give advice on the purchase of hardware, the first expectation of classteachers is that their IT coordinator should know all about the software packages currently in school. New to the post, you will need to build up a knowledge of the school's stock of programs. Some of this can be done by collating information already available about regularly used programs. A simple index box will suit your purpose. However, it will be the pile of unmarked discs and lost manuals separated from their discs which will cause any newcomer to the job to despair in the first few weeks.

Firstly don't panic

If the school has been able to manage with such chaos over a number of years then a few more months won't matter. Recruit any sympathetic teachers to help you discover what you do have in the school and how useful it is. Buy some labels and use them to identify discs. Distribute two or three discs at a time to your colleagues and ask them to write on the labels in felt pen (biros may damage the discs). Negotiate a deadline for each little task or you may be hindered rather than helped in this exercise. In this way you will start to make sense of the multiple versions, damaged discs and pirate copies which no doubt will be present in the pile. Destroy any copyright material which you suspect to be pirate copies. You do not want the first money you manage to obtain to go on the payment of fines for breach of copyright.

Secondly attempt to match the discs with their booklets
The accompanying documentation which publishers supply with their software will vary in quality, quantity and type. It is a rare booklet that is of no use to anyone — unless, of course, it is separated from its disc. You should ensure that packages returned to you do still have the documentation.

Thirdly keep a record of what you have found
Use your index file. You will then be on your way to organising the resources such that they will be of use to people. At first you may wish just to record these and catalogue them alphabetically. Later, as you will have seen some of the software in action, you may choose to create a catalogue in terms of age suitability.

Some of the discs you find will be master copies and these should not be used by the children. Make backup copies of these and lock the originals away securely. Be assured that the first time you decide that it will not matter if you use the master copy for once — it will! The organisation of access to software is a perennial problem for coordinators. You may come up with ingenious solutions but in the main you have three basic choices:

- Keep discs and associated documentation centrally. Give a copy of the list of programs to each teacher. When any class teacher wants to use a particular disc, book it out to them. Keep backup copies in a separate place in order to take account of accidental damage to discs.

- Make multiple copies of popular programs so that each teacher can have his or her own. You will need to consider whether to make copies of the handbook where allowed, for each teacher.
- Issue discs to the most suitable class or department keeping a note of who has what. The locations of the discs will have to be issued to all teachers by means of a general list. Frequent checks will need to be made of the discs and documentation. **Remember, never give anyone a copy of a master disc**.

The system you choose will need to account for the types of computer in your school, the convenience of a location for central storage, the popularity of certain programs and whether you have site licence or single copy software.

Most important is the quality of information teachers have to hand about the software available. Hopefully, your school will have purchased software which includes much of this in the accompanying documentation. Whether this is the case or not, it will prove a worthwhile investment to buy folders for each of your main programs into which are put both the disc and accompanying booklet with examples of use by teachers in your school. Clear plastic foolscap folders with zip openings are best for this job in order that contents are visible. The graphs children have drawn using data handling packages, fancy lettering used in stories children might have written, a teacher's jotting on the work children did as a result of an adventure program, are all examples of items teachers would find useful to be included in such envelopes.

This is merely an extension of the 'pooling' of topic worksheets which goes on in many schools, but by creating browsable packages you may make a contribution to a change in some teachers' use of ICT.

As you develop your role you may wish to be more proactive in the way you distribute software to various classes.

Free choice in the use of software may be your most appropriate strategy. If new to the school you might quite naturally feel it to be difficult to assert that teacher X cannot use package Y with her class, even if there are excellent reasons for this decision. In addition, if the use of computers is somewhat spasmodic in your school then putting obstacles in the way of staff is clearly not the way in which to promote increased usage and to persuade teachers that using ICT in their teaching will be painless and beneficial for their children.

It may be possible to persuade teacher X that package Z more closely fits her needs. Thus we move to the situation where software is assigned to different areas of the school, in the hope that this will contribute to a progression in skill development — more sophisticated software with more facilities being provided for older children. The ultimate goal is for such skills to take the centre stage and teachers use aspects of different software to enhance this learning. Once such a move has been established and teachers are used to planning children's ICT work in this way, then moving back to free choice may again be most appropriate.

Knowing what is available outside the school is a longer-term task. Sending for catalogues from software manufactures may be a good start.

Ablac Learning Works South Devon House Newton Abbot Devon TQ12 2BP	**Aptech Ltd** Aptech House Ponteland Newcastle upon Tyne NE20 9SD	**Argo Interactive Group** 7 Dukes Court Chichester West Sussex, PO19 2FX	**Aspex Software** Heather Down Road Tavistock Devon PL19 9AG
Awesome Ideas PO Box 402 Bradford BD9 5YL Tel.: 01274 480067	**Brilliant Computing,** PO Box 142, Bradford, West Yorkshire BD9 5NF Tel.: 01274 497617/578239	**Claris International Inc,** Meadowbank Furlong Road Bourne End SL8 5AJ Tel.: 01628 534100	**Crick Software** 1 Avenue, Spinney Hill, Northampton NN3 6BA Tel.: 01604 671691

Don Johnston Special Needs 18 Clarenden Court Winwick Quay Warrington WA2 8QP	**Dorling Kindersley** 9 Henrietta Street Covent Garden London WC2 8PS	**ESM,** 2nd Floor, Abbeygate House, East road Cambridge CB1 1BG	**4mationEducational Software,** 14 Castle Park Rd Barnstaple, Devon, EX32 8PA Tel.: 01271 325353
Fisher-Marriott Software, 3 Grove Road, Ansty, Coventry CV7 9JD Tel.: 01203 616325	**Ginn & Co. Ltd,** Prebendal House, Parson's Fee, Aylesbury, Buckinghamshire, HP20 2QZ Tel.: 01296 488411	**Icon Technology Ltd,** Church House, Church Street, Carlby Stanford, Lincs PE9 4NB Tel.: 0116 2546225	**International Thomson Publishing Services,** Cheriton House, North Way, Andover, Hants SP10 5BE Tel.: 01264 332424
ITMA, The Shell Centre of Mathematical Education, The University, Nottingham, NG7 2RD	**Kudlian Soft,** 8 Barrow Road, Kenilworth, Warwickshire CV8 1EH Tel.: 01926 842544	**Longman Logotron,** 124 Cambridge Science Park, Milton Road, Cambridge CB4 4ZS Tel.: 01223 425558	**MAPE,** Newman College, Bartley Green, Birmingham, B32 3NT
Oak Solutions Ltd, Dial House, 12 Chapel Street, Halton, Leeds LS15 7RN Tel.: 0113 2326992	**Potential Software** Treidar farm Wendron Helston TR13 0NL	**Resource** The Resource centre 51 High Street Kegworth Derbyshire DE74 2DA	**School's direct CD-ROM** The Green Ravesthorpe Northampton NN6 8EP
Sibelius Software 75 Burleigh Street Cambridge CB1 1DJ Tel.: 01223 302765	**Sherston Software** Ltd, Angel House, Sherston, Malmesbury, Wilts SN16 0LH Tel.: 01666 840433	**Smile Mathematics** Isaac Newton PDC 108A leicester Rd London W11 1QS	**Softline** Mill House Mill Lane Carshalton Surrey SM5 2WZ
Stanley Thornes Publishing Ellenborough House Wellington Street Cheltenham GL50 1YD	**Tag Developments** 19 High Street Gravesend Kent DA11 0BA	**Thomas Nelson and Sons Ltd.,** Nelson House, Mayfield Road, Walton-on-Thames Surrey KT12 5PL Tel.: 01932 252211	**USBOURNE Publishing** 6 Euston Street Freemans Common Leicester LE2 7SS
Volnet Multimedia Centre 3 Devonshire St London W1N 2BA	**White Space** 48 St Dunstan's Road London W6 8RE Tel.: 0181 748 5927	**Widgit Software,** 102 Radford Road Leamington Spa, Warwickshire CV31 1LF Tel.: 01926 885303	**YITM** 1 Broadbent Road Oldham Manchester Tel.: 0161 627 4469

IT coordinators will also need to consider CD ROM titles and make recommendations to other coordinatotrs to ensure that they offer educational value for money. NCET have carried out a number of surveys and the results have been published. In this example they offer some practical advice to coordinators who intend to review and choose their own titles.

> *It is important to remember that CD ROM titles come in several different guises. Multimedia titles, with their engaging combination of text, audio, animation and video, are very expensive to develop and consequently expensive to buy. Resource banks of images or full-text databases of newspapers provide huge storehouse of information, but without sophisticated information skills students may not necessarily retrieve the information they require; too much information can present as much of a problem as too little. Discs designed for home use such as talking story books, can be used successfully at school especially if learning support materials are developed to focus their use.*

While you may be able to read educational reviews of a range of CD ROM titles, there is no substitute for examining it for yourself. Many publishers provide CD ROMs on approval and LEA IT centres may be able to lend you one. Consider:

- Does it fit well with the curriculum?
- When was it published?
- What is the balance of text, illustrations, audio and video?
- Is the vocabulary, structure and sentence length suitable?
- Is there an audio option and can the volume be controlled?
- Can you print and save selected pictures and text?
- Will children be able to find their way around easily?
- Does it have a built-in dictionary or glossary?

Several software companies listed above include CD ROMs within their software catalogues.

Some titles	Producers
Usborne Exploring Nature, *HMTC* Dictionary of the Living World, *Media Design Interactive* The Way Things Work, *Dorling Kindersley* Microsoft Dinosaurs, *Microsoft* Talking First World for Windows *Research Machines* A to Zap!, *TAG Developments Ltd* Information finder: World Book Encyclopaedia, *World Book Childcraft International*	**HMTC** (distributor for Main Multimedia), Connaught Lane, Paulsgrove, Portsmouth PO6 4SJ Tel.: 01705 378266 **Dorling Kindersley Multimedia**, 36–38 West Street, London WC2H 9NA Tel.: 0171 8365411 **World Book Childcraft International**, World Book House, 77 Mount Ephraim, Tunbridge Wells, Kent TN4 8AZ **Media Design Interactive**, The Old Hop Kiln, 1 Long Garden Walk, Farnham, Surrey GU9 7HP Tel.: 01252 737630 **Research Machines plc**, New Mill House, 183 Milton Park, Abingdon, Oxford OX14 4SE Tel.: 01235 826000; 01235 826868

NCET: Choosing and Using IT gives further information on CD ROMs. It is published by

Contact

National Council for Educational Technology
Milburn Hill Road,
Science Park,
Coventry CV4 7JJ.

IT coordinators might like to guide trips from your school towards places which have computer displays. Several sites help children gain an understanding of the ways computers can be used in society. Some of the following **Interactive Science and Technology Centres** listed in Newton and Newton (1998) might prove useful to check if they can meet the objectives of your next school trip.

Interactive Science and Technology Centres		
Launch Pad Science Museum, Exhibition Road, London SW7 2DD	***Xperiment!*** Greater Manchester Museum of Science and Industry, Castlefield, Manchester M3 4JP	***Science Factory*** Newcastle Museum of Science and Engineering, Blandford Street, Newcastle upon Tyne NE1 4JA
BNFL, Community Affairs, Risley, Warrington, Cheshire WA3 9AS Tel.: 01925–832826	***Discovery Dome*** c/o Science Projects, Turnham Green, Terrace Mews, London W1 1QU	***Technology Testbed*** National Museums and Galleries on Merseyside, Large Objects Collection, Princes Dock, Pier Head, Liverpool L3 0AA
Glasgow Dome of Discovery South Rotunda, 100 Govan Road, Glasgow G51 1JS	***Light on Science*** Birmingham Museum of Science and Industry, Newhall Street, Birmingham B3 1RX	***The Exploratory*** The Old Station, Temple Meads, Bristol BS8 1QU

Several organisations and associated journals are either directly concerned with IT in education or regularly publish articles and helpful advice.

Contact

ACITT: National Association for Co-ordinators and Teachers of IT
Brondale Cottage
5 Spring Gardens, Narberth
Dyfed SA67 7BN Tel.: 01474 332791
http://www.acitt.org.uk/

British Association of Early Childhood Education (BAECE)
111 City View House
463 Bethnal Green Road
London E2 9QY
Tel.: 0171 739 7594

Early Childhood Education Forum
c/o Gillian Pugh
National Children's Bureau
8mWakley Street
London EC1V 7Q6
Tel.: 0171 843 6000 Fax: 0171 278 9512

Institute of Food Science and Technology
5 Cambridge Court
210 Shepherd's Bush Road
London W6 7NL
Tel.: 0171 603 6316

Micros and Primary Education (MAPE)
The Old Vicarage Skegby Road
Normanton-on-Trent
Nottinghamshire
NG23 6BR
Tel.: 01636 821647

National Association of Advisers & Inspectors in Design & Technology (NAAIDT)
124 Kidmore Road
Caversham
Reading
Berkshire RG4 7NB
Tel.: 01734 470615 Fax: 1734 470615

Amateur Music Association
30 Park Drive
Grimsby
South Humberside
DN32 0EG
Tel.: 01472 78002

Department of Education and Employment (DFEE)
Sanctuary Buildings
Great Smith Street London
SW1P 3BT Tel.: 0171 925 5000
http://www/open.gov.uk/dfee/dfeehome.htm

Information Technology in Teacher Education Assn (ITTE)
Brighton University
School of Education
Falmer Brighton BN1 9PH
Tel.: 01273 643423

Learning for Life (LIFT)
PO Box 1577
London
W7 2ZT

Music Masters' and Mistresses' Association
Three Ways
Chicks Lane
Kilndown, Goodhurst
Kent TN17 2RS
Tel.: 01892 890537 Fax: 01892 890537

National Association of Advisors for Computers in Education (NAACE)
PO Box 60
Tipton West Midlands DY4 0YS
Tel.: 0121 530 9732 Fax: 0121 530 9732
Email: mikesmith@rmplc.co.uk
http://www.naace.org

National Association of Design Education
26 Dorchester Close
Mansfield
Nottinghamshire NG18 4QW
Tel.: 01628 631551

National Early Years Network
77 Holloway Road
London
N7 8JZ
Tel.: 0171 607 9573

National Primary Centre
Westminster College
Oxford
OX2 9AT
Tel.: 01865 245242

Office for Standards in Education (OFSTED)
Alexandra House
29 Kingsway
London WC2B 6SE
Tel.: 0171 421 6800 Fax: 0171 421 6707
URL: http://www.open.gov.uk/ofsted/ofsted.htm

Preschool Learning Alliance
National Centre
69 Kings Cross Road
London WC1X 9LL
Tel.: 0171 833 0991 Fax: 0171 837 4942

Reading and Language Information Centre
University of Reading
Bulmershe Court
Reading RG56 1HY
Tel.: 01189 318820

Scottish Council for Educational Technology (SCET)
Dowanhill
74 Victoria Crescent Road
Glasgow G12 9JN
Tel.: 0141 337 5000 Fax: 0141 337 5050
http://www.scet.com/

National Association of Music Advisers (NAME)
County Music Centre Westfield Primary School
Bonsey Lane
Westfield, Woking
Surrey GU22 9PR Tel.: 01483 728711

National Foundation for Educational Research in England and Wales (NFER)
The Mere Upton Park
Slough Berkshire SL1 2DQ
Tel.: 01753 574123 Fax: 01753 691632

National Society for Education in Art and Design (NSEAD)
The Gatehouse Corsham Court
Corsham Wiltshire
SN13 0BZ Tel.: 01249 714825

Parents Information Network (PIN)
PO Box 1577
London
W7 3ZT
Tel.: 0181 248 4666 Fax: 0181 566 3336

Qualifications and Curriculum Authority (OCA)
Newcombe House
45 Notting Hill Gate London W11 3JB
Tel.: 0171 229 1234 Fax: 0171 229 8526
http://www.open.gov.uk/qca/index.htm

Royal Society of Arts (RSA)
Examinations Board
Westwood Way
Coventry CV4 8HS
Tel.: 01203 470033 Fax: 01203 468080

Sonic Arts Network
London House
271–273 King Street
London
W6 9LZ
Tel.: 0181 741 7422 Fax: 0181 741 7433

Teacher Training Agency (TTA)
Portland House Stag Place
London SW1E 5TT
Tel.: 0171 925 3728
http://www/coi.gov.uk/coi/depts/GTT/GTT.html

Textile Institute
10 Blackfriars Street
Manchester
M3 5DR
Tel.: 0161 834 8457 Fax: 0161 835 3087

The Design and Technology Association (DATA)
16 Wellesbourne House
Walton Road
Wellesbourne Warwich CV35 9JB
Tel.: 01789 470007 Fax: 01789 841955

The Design Council Education and Training Foundation
1 Oxendon Street
London SW1Y 4EE
Tel.: 0171 208 2121 Fax: 0171 839 6033

UK Council for Music Education and Training
13 Back Lane
South Luffenham
Oakham
Rutland LE15 8NQ
Tel.: 01780 721115 Fax: 01780 721401

Journals

Art and Craft Design Technology
Scholastic Publications — monthly

British Journal of Educational Technology (BJET)
Blackwells — 3 issues per year

CD ROM Magazine
Dennis Publishing Ltd, monthly

Computer Music Journal
Massachusetts Institute of Technology (MIT) ISSN: 01489267 — quarterly

Computer Shopper
Dennis Publishing Ltd, ISSN: 09558578, monthly

Design and Technology Teaching
DATA — 3 issues per year

Educational Computing & Technology
Training Information Network — 8 issues per year

Envision
NCET, ISSN: 13589865 — 3 issues per year

Interactive: Learning with Information Technology
Questions Publishing, ISSN: 13601954, bi-monthly

Music Teacher
Rhinegold Publishing — monthly

PC guide [previous title: CD ROM today]
Future Publishing — monthly

Sound on Sound
SOS Publications, ISSN: 09516816, — monthly

Technology in Music Education
Oscar Music and Media — 6 issues per year

Personal Computer World
VNU Business Publications, ISSN: 01420232 — monthly

Technology in Education
B & S Publications — 7 issues per year*

Times Educational Supplement
The Times — weekly

When advising teachers about ICT issues in mathematics education useful publications are issued by:

Contact

Association of Teachers of Mathematics,
7 Shaftesbury Street,
Derby,
DE3 8YB

The Mathematical Association, has an address at:
259, London Rd,
Leicester
LE2 3BE

World Wide Web Addresses for maths education, in addition to those found in chapter 5:

Brian Teasers http://www.geocities.com/Athens/Parthenon/4046/
Freudenthal Institute http://www.fi.ruu.nl
Fun With Numbers http://www.newdream.net/~sage/old/numbers/
Great Penny Toss http://192.246.43.96/RBS_Forms/Rbs.html
Maths enrichment http://nrich.maths.org.uk/
Maths forum http://www.forum.swarthmore.edu/
Maths links http://www.chester.ac.uk/~mwillard/teacher_education/homepage.htm
Tessalations http://www.mcs.net/#highland/tess/tess.html

Other Useful web pages

Arizona Health Sciences Library
http://ahsc.arizona.edu/

Antique Roman Dishes
http://www.cs.cmu.edu/~mjw/recipes/ethnic/historical/

Biotech in a Bag
http://www.gene.com/ae/ab/

Centre for Alternative Technology
http://www.cat.org.uk/

D&T Online
http://www.dtonline.org/

Design Council
http://www.design-council.org.uk/

How Batteries Work
http://www.duracellusa.com/Spp/Battery/how.html

Illustrated Tour of Thermoplastics
http://www.ge.com/plastics/educate/gpdes00.htm

Institute of Food Science and Technology Homepage
http://www.easynet.co.uk/ifst/ifsthp3.htm

On-line reviews of over 600 educational CD-ROM titles
http://www.ncet.org.uk/cd-rom.html

UK Technology Education Centre
http://www.technologyindex.com/education/

Further reading on issues covered in this book:

Contact

Portable Computers in Action, NCET, 1994, £5.00 ISBN 1 85379 311 6

Portable Computers Pilot Evaluation Summary, NCET, 1994, £2.50 ISBN 1 85379 301 9

SITSS (Shropshire Information Technology Support Services), Bourne House, Radbrook Centre, Radbrook, Shrewsbury SY3 9BJ Tel.: 01743 246043

Advisory Unit: Computers in Education, 126 Great North Road, Hatfield, Herts AL9 5JZ Tel.: 01707 266714

References

ACITT (1995) 'The buffer's guide to the Internet', *Integrate 20/ art 11.*

ACITT (1996) 'Net Supervision', *Integrate 20/ art 21.*

AINLEY, J. (1997) *Enriching Primary Mathematics with IT*, London, Hodder and Stoughton.

ALEXANDER, R., ROSE, J. and WOODHEAD, C. (1992) *Curriculum Organisation and Classroom Practice in Primary Schools*, London: HMSO.

BARBER, M. (1994) 'Keep the new light burning brightly', *TES*, 9.9.94.

BELL, D. (1992) 'Coordinating science in primary schools: a role model?', *Evaluation and Research in Education*, **6**, 2–3, pp. 155–171.

BLEASE, D. and LEVER, D. (1992) 'What do primary headteachers really do?', *Educational Studies*, **8**, 2, 1992.

BIRMINGHAM, LEA (1996) *Primary Planning Project*, Birmingham City Council.

BOWLES, G. (1989) 'Marketing and promotion', in FIDLER, B. and BOWLES, G. (eds) *Effective Local Management of Schools* (BEMAS), Longman: Essex.

BROWN, C., BARNFIELD, J. and STONE, M. (1990) *A Spanner in the Works: Primary School Teaching for Equality and Justice*, Trentham Books: Stoke-on-Trent.

CAMPBELL, R. J. (1985) *Developing the Primary School Curriculum*, London: Holt Saunders.

CAMPBELL, R. J. and NEILL, S. R. (1994) *Primary Teachers at Work*, London: Routledge.

CLEMSON, D. (1996) 'Information technology in the National Curriculum', in COULBY, D. and WARD, S. (eds) *The Primary Core National Curriculum*, London: Cassell.

COCKCROFT, W. (1982) *Mathematics Counts*, London: HMSO.

COUPLAND, J. (1995) *Choosing IT Support and Services*, Coventry: NCET.

COX, M. et al. (1988) 'The use of computer assisted learning in primary schools: some factors affecting uptake', *Computer Education*, **12**, 1, pp. 173–178.

COX, M. and RHODES, V. (1988) 'Training primary school teachers to use computers effectively in classrooms', Conference paper for Technology in Education, 29–31 March, 1998.

CROMPTON, R. and MANN, P. (1996) *IT across the Curriculum*, London: Cassell.

CROSS, A. and BIRCH, A. (1995) *Portable Computers Portable Learning: An Evaluation of the Use of Portable Computers in Primary Years*, Department of Education, University of Manchester.

CROSS, A. and CROSS, S. V. (1994) 'Organising a professional development day for your colleagues', in HARRISON, M. (ed.) *Beyond the Core Curriculum*, Plymouth: Northcote House.

CROSS, A. and HARRISON, M. (1994) 'Successful curriculum change through coordination', in HARRISON, M. (ed.) *Beyond the Core Curriculum*, Plymouth: Northcote House.

DAUITE, C. (1992) 'Multimedia composing: extending the resources of kindergarten to writers across the grades', *Language Arts*, **69**, 4, pp. 250–260.

DAVIES, J. (1990) *Working with Colleagues: Supporting Primary Maths*, Milton Keynes: Centre for Mathematics Education at the Open University.

DAVIS, N., DESFORGE, C., JESSEL, J., SOMEKH, B., TAYLOR, C. and VAUGHAN, G. (1992) 'Can Quality in Learning be Enhanced through the use of IT?' *Developing Information Technology in Teacher Education*, **5** May.

DEAN, J. (1987) *Managing the Primary School*, Kent: Croome Helme.

DEAN, G. (1996) 'Inspecting IT', *Interactive*, December 1996, pp. 17–19.

Dempsey, J. (1995) 'Using IT in music', in Donnelly, J. (ed.) *IT in Schools*, Buckingham: The Questions Publishing Co.

DES (1978) *Primary Education in England*, London: HMSO.

DES (1982) *Mathematics Counts — the Cockcroft Report*, London: HMSO.

DES (1988) *Conditions of Service*, London: HMSO.

DES (1990) *HMCI Annual Report*, London: HMSO.

Devereux, J. (1991) 'Using IT, other than computers, to support primary science', *Primary Science Review*, 20 Dec. 1991.

DfEE (1997) *Connecting the Learning Society: National Grid for Learning*, London: DfEE.

Donnelly, J. (1995) 'The role of the head teacher and senior management team', in Donnelly, J. (ed.) *IT in Schools*, Buckingham: The Questions Publishing Co.

Drage, C. (1995) 'First steps with a tiny robot', *TES*, 6th January, 1995.

Edwards, A. (1993) 'Curriculum coordination: a lost opportunity for primary schools', *School Organisation*, **13**, 1, pp. 51–59.

Edwards, A. (1997) 'Manifesto for computer literacy', *TES*, 28th February, 1997.

Erault, M. and Hoyles, C. (1989) 'Groupwork with computers', *Journal of Computer Assisted Learning*, **5**, 1, pp. 12–24.

Essex County Council (1996) *The Information Technology Handbook*, Essex County Council: Ilford.

Fisher, E. (1993) 'The teacher's role', in Scrimshaw, P. (ed.) *Language, Classrooms and Computers*, London: Routledge.

Fullan, M. and Hargreaves, A. (1992) *What's Worth Fighting For in Your School?*, Buckingham: Open University Press.

Gadsby, P. and Harrison, M. (1998) *Ofsted Re-inspection and the Subject Coordinators*, London: Falmer Press.

Gaine, C. (1987) *No Problem Here*, London: Hutchinson.

Galton, M. (1995) *Crisis in the Primary Classroom*, London: David Fulton.

Govier, H. (1994) 'An IT Policy Document', *Micros in Primary Education*, Autumn 1994.

Haigh, G. (1994) 'Principle governing purchase', *TES*, 7th October, 1994.

HARRINGTON, H. (1992) 'Fostering critical reflection through technology: preparing prospective teachers for a changing society', *Journal of Information Technology for Teacher Education*, **1**, 1.

HARRISON, M. (1994) 'Teachers computers and the curriculum: the three roles of the primary IT coordinator', in HARRISON, M. (ed.) *Beyond the Core Curriculum*, Plymouth: Northcote House.

HARRISON, M. (1994b) 'Time to debunk the glorious past', *TES*, 24.06.94.

HARRISON, M. (1994c) 'Towards Education for all: Using computers as a tool', in PUMFREY, P. and VERMA, G. (eds) *Cultural Diversity and the National Curriculum: Volume 4: Cross Curricular elements in the Primary School*, London: Falmer Press.

HARRISON, M. A. and GILL, S. C. (1992) *Primary School Management*, London: Heinemann.

HARRISON, S. and THEAKER, K. (1989) *Curriculum Leadership and Coordination in the Primary School*, Whalley, Guild House Press.

HILL, J. (1990) 'Children in control', *Teachers' Voices 2, Palm Project*, Coventry, NCET.

HOLLY, P. and SOUTHWORTH, G. (1989) *The Developing School*, London: Falmer.

HORBY, A. and PEARS, H. (1994) 'Collaborative groupwork: how infant children can manage IT', *Education*, 3–13, October 1994.

HOWARD, B. (1993) 'Building self esteem', *Micromaths*, Summer 1993, pp. 31–35.

HOYLES, C. (1988) 'Review of the literature', in HOYLES, C. (ed.) *Girls and Computers*, Bedford Way Papers, 34, University of London.

HOYLES, C. and SUTHERLAND, R. (1989) LOGO *Mathematics in the Classroom*, London: Routledge.

JESSEL, J. (1992) 'Do children really use the word processor as a thought processor?' *Developing Information Technology in Teacher Education*, **5**, May, pp. 23–32.

JOY, J., HARTLAND, S. and TOLLEY, J. (1992) *Bright Ideas: Computer Activities*, Leamington Spa: Scholastic Publications.

JUDD, J. (1991) *Children Computers and the National Curriculum*, Coventry: NCET.

KOTLER, P. and FOX, K. (1985) *Strategic Marketing for Educational Institutions*, New York: Prentice Hall.

LIGHT, P. (1993) 'Collaborative learning with computers', in SCRIMSHAW, P. (ed.) *Language, Classrooms and Computers*, London: Routledge.

MAILER, N. and DICKSON, B. (1996) *The UK Internet Primer*, Birmingham: The Questions Publishing Co.

MCTAGGART, M. (1997) 'Palms take root in East London', *TES*, 20th June, 1997.

MEADOWS, J. (1992) 'International collaborations in teacher education: a constructivist approach to using electronic mail for communication in partnership with schools', *Journal of Information Technology for Teacher Education*, **1**, 1.

MERCER, N. (1994) 'The quality of talk in children's joint activity at the computer', *Journal of Computer Assisted Learning*, **10**, pp. 24–32.

MESSER, D. and LIGHT, P. (1991) 'The role of collaboration and feedback in children's computer based learning', *Journal of Computer Assisted Learning*, **7**, 2, pp. 156–159.

MOORE, J. L. (1992) 'The role of the science co-ordinator in primary schools: a survey of headteachers' views', *School Organisation*, **12**, 1, pp. 7–15.

MOORE, J. L. (1994) 'Activity groupings of primary science co-ordinators: a survey of co-ordinators' activities', *Research in Science and Technological Education*, **12**, 1, pp. 15–20.

NCET (1992) *Assessing IT — Curriculum Support Materials*, Coventry: NCET.

NCET (1993) *Seen IT in the UK*, Coventry: NCET.

NCET (1994) *Portable Computers in Action*, Coventry: NCET.

NCET (1995) *IT Helps: Using It to Support Basic Literacy and Numeracy*, Coventry: NCET.

NCET (1996) *Primary Music — A Pupil's Entitlement to IT*, Coventry: NCET.

NCET (1996) *Chosy & Using IT*, Coventry: NCET.

NCET (1997) *Reviewing IT*, Coventry: NCET.

NCET/NAACE (1992) *Inspecting IT — Support Materials*, Coventry: NCET.

NEWTON, L. and NEWTON, G. (1998) *Coordinating science across the Primary School*, London: Falmer Press.

NIAS, J., SOUTHWORTH, G. W. and YEOMANS, R. (1989) *Staff Relationships in the Primary School: A Study of Organisational Cultures*, London: Cassell.

NOVAK, J. D. and GOWIN, D. B. (1984) *Learning How to Learn*, New York: Cambridge University Press.

OFSTED (1994) *Primary Matters: A Discussion on Teaching and Learning in Primary Schools*, London: OFSTED.

OFSTED (1995) *Information Technology: A Review of Inspection Findings*, London: HMSO.

O'NEILL, J. (1996) *Effective Curriculum Management*, London: Routledge.

OWEN, G. (1992) 'Whole-school management of information technology', *School Organisation*, **12**, 1.

PAISLEY, A. and PAISLEY, A. (1989) *Effective Management in Primary Schools*, Oxford: Basil Blackwell.

PALMER, S. (1997) 'The matter is in hand', *TES*, 14th February, 1997.

PICKARD, W. (1997) '*Negativity of the Net, TES*, 27th June, 1997.

PLAYFOOT, D., SKELTON, M. and SOUTHWORTH, G. (1989) *The Primary School Management Book*, London: Mary Glasgow Publishers Limited.

RAGSDALE, R. G. (1991) 'Effective computing in education: teachers' tools and training', *Education and Computing*, **7**, pp. 157–166.

ROBERTS, G. (1985) 'The organisation of learning in primary schools. Memorandum 50', in *Achievement in Primary Schools*, London: HMSO.

SCAA (1997) *Expectations in Information Technology at Key Stages 1 and 2*, London: SCAA.

SHAN, S. J. and BAILEY, P. (1991) *Multiple Factors: Classroom Mathematics for Equality and Justice*, Trentham Books: Stoke-on-Trent.

SHEPHARD, G. (1997) *Press Release*, 18 Feb. 1992, DfEE.

SMITH, H. (1996) *The Really Practical Guide to Primary RE*, London: Stanley Thornes.

SMITHERS, A. and ZIENTEK, P. (1991) *Gender, Primary Schools and the National Curriculum*, Birmingham: NASUWT and the Engineering Council.

SOMETIH, B. (1989) 'Teachers becoming researchers', Paper for NECC conference, Boston Massachusetts.

SOMEKH, B. and DAVIES, R. (1991) 'Towards a pedagogy for information technology', *The Curriculum Journal*, **2**, 2, Spring 1991, pp. 153–170.

STRAKER, A. (1989) *Children Using Computers*, Oxford: Blackwell.

STRAKER, A. and GOVIER, H. (1996) *Children Using Computers*, Oxford: Blackwell.

TAGG, B. (1996) 'The school in an information age', in TAGG, B. (ed.) *Developing a Whole-school IT Policy*, London: Pitman.

VERMA, G. K. (1993) 'Cultural diversity in secondary schools: its nature, extent and curricular implications', in PUMFREY, P. and VERMA, G. K. (eds) *Cultural Diversity and the Curriculum: Volume 1, The Foundation Subjects and Religious Education in Secondary Schools*, London: The Falmer Press, pp. 15–27.

VERMA, G. K. (1993b) 'Cultural diversity in secondary schools: its nature, extent and cross-curricular implications', in VERMA, G. K. and PUMFREY, P. (eds) *Cultural Diversity and the Curriculum: Volume 2, Cross-curricular contexts, Themes and Dimensions in Secondary Schools*, London: The Falmer Press, pp. 32–42.

WALKER, T. (1995) 'Sounding the right note', in HARRISON, M. (ed.) *Developing a Leadership Role in the Key Stage 2 Curriculum*, London: Falmer Press.

WATSON, D. (1993) *The Impact Report*, London: Kings College.

WEBB, R. (1994) *After the Deluge: Changing Roles and Responsibilities in the Primary School*, London.

WEBB, R. and VULLIAMY, G. (1994) 'The changing role of the primary school coordinator', *The Curriculum Journal*, **6**, 1.

WEST-BURNHAM, J. (1997) *Managing Quality in Schools: Effective Strategies for Quality Based School Improvement*, London: Pitman.

WORTLEY, B. (1993) 'The role of subject coordinators in primary schools: the state of the art', *Education Today*, **43**, 1, pp. 43–48.

YELLAND, N. J. (1994) 'The strategies and interactions of young children in LOGO tasks', *Journal of Computer Assisted Learning*, 16, pp. 34–49.

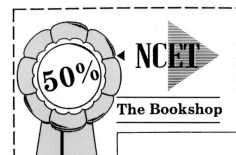

Index